GUIDANCE ON ENSURING CONTROL ROOM OPERATOR (CRO) COMPETENCE

1st edition

December 2014

Published by
ENERGY INSTITUTE, LONDON
The Energy Institute is a professional membership body incorporated by Royal Charter 2003
Registered charity number 1097899

The Energy Institute (EI) is the chartered professional membership body for the energy industry, supporting over 20 000 individuals working in or studying energy and 250 energy companies worldwide. The EI provides learning and networking opportunities to support professional development, as well as professional recognition and technical and scientific knowledge resources on energy in all its forms and applications.

The EI's purpose is to develop and disseminate knowledge, skills and good practice towards a safe, secure and sustainable energy system. In fulfilling this mission, the EI addresses the depth and breadth of the energy sector, from fuels and fuels distribution to health and safety, sustainability and the environment. It also informs policy by providing a platform for debate and scientifically-sound information on energy issues.

The EI is licensed by:
- the Engineering Council to award Chartered, Incorporated and Engineering Technician status;
- the Science Council to award Chartered Scientist status, and
- the Society for the Environment to award Chartered Environmentalist status.

It also offers its own Chartered Energy Engineer, Chartered Petroleum Engineer and Chartered Energy Manager titles.

A registered charity, the EI serves society with independence, professionalism and a wealth of expertise in all energy matters.

This publication has been produced as a result of work carried out within the Technical Team of the EI, funded by the EI's Technical Partners. The EI's Technical Work Programme provides industry with cost-effective, value-adding knowledge on key current and future issues affecting those operating in the energy sector, both in the UK and internationally.

For further information, please visit **http://www.energyinst.org**

The EI gratefully acknowledges the financial contributions towards the scientific and technical programme from the following companies

BG Group	Premier Oil
BP Exploration Operating Co Ltd	RWE npower
BP Oil UK Ltd	Saudi Aramco
Centrica	Scottish Power
Chevron	SGS
ConocoPhillips Ltd	Shell UK Oil Products Limited
Dana Petroleum	Shell U.K. Exploration and Production Ltd
DONG Energy	SSE
EDF Energy	Statkraft
ENI	Statoil
E. ON UK	Talisman Sinopec Energy UK Ltd
ExxonMobil International Ltd	Total E&P UK Limited
International Power	Total UK Limited
Kuwait Petroleum International Ltd	Tullow
Maersk Oil North Sea UK Limited	Valero
Murco Petroleum Ltd	Vattenfall
Nexen	Vitol
Phillips 66	World Fuel Services

However, it should be noted that the above organisations have not all been directly involved in the development of this publication, nor do they necessarily endorse its content.

ISBN 978 0 85293 724 2

Published by the Energy Institute

The information contained in this publication is provided for general information purposes only. Whilst the Energy Institute and the contributors have applied reasonable care in developing this publication, no representations or warranties, express or implied, are made by the Energy Institute or any of the contributors concerning the applicability, suitability, accuracy or completeness of the information contained herein and the Energy Institute and the contributors accept no responsibility whatsoever for the use of this information. Neither the Energy Institute nor any of the contributors shall be liable in any way for any liability, loss, cost or damage incurred as a result of the receipt or use of the information contained herein.

Hard copy and electronic access to EI and IP publications is available via our website, **www.energypublishing.org**. Documents can be purchased online as downloadable pdfs or on an annual subscription for single users and companies. For more information, contact the EI Publications Team.

e: **pubs@energyinst.org**

CONTENTS

Contents continued   Page

Contents continued   Page

FOREWORD

Control room operators (CROs) perform a critical role in running normal operations, infrequent activities such as process shut downs, and handling abnormal events and emergencies. Ensuring a sufficient number of competent CROs are available on site is a key element of safety, and can contribute positively to productivity. CROs include people who work fulltime in control rooms, people who have an occasional control room role and control room supervisors or technicians who may need to engage with CROs in specific circumstances.

There are many guides and standards on competence management in safety critical industries. However, this publication provides specific guidance on how to assure competence of CROs in the energy industries, particularly how to define competence standards, select training and development methods, assess CROs and maintain their competence once in post. The guidance is consistent with common models of competence management, but offers guidance that is specific to CROs.

Feedback from industry indicates that there are some particular issues with respect to CROs. There are challenges in achieving an adequate pool of candidates from which to select CROs and challenges in retaining CROs once they are in post. Therefore, this guide goes beyond common competence management guidance to cover these important challenges.

CROs are often selected from field operators, drawing on their experience and knowledge of the plant. This has a major implication; the recruitment of field operators should foresee the subsequent requirement for CROs. This guide therefore advises that at least some field operators are recruited based on their potential to be CROs. Methods of assessing underpinning skills are cited in the guide to help identify potential CROs amongst current or candidate field operators. Given that people do not become established CROs overnight, an incremental approach to competence development is needed, progressing from beginners to established and then to advanced CROs. Guidance is provided on the formulation of an incremental approach to development, combining taught and structured on the job learning.

There are many aspects of retaining people. This guide firstly focuses on providing CROs with a structured route for advancement, providing people with the scope for further development once they are in post. Learning and further qualification opportunities may be provided and CROs encouraged and enabled to make use of these opportunities. In addition, creating a positive working environment through practical procedures, ergonomic equipment, supportive supervision and change management all contribute to staff retention as well as help reduce operator error.

This guide presents a full lifecycle view of CROs, from the creation of a pool of candidates to advancement of their competence when in post. Extensive annexes provide practical tools, such as checklists for assessing the organisation's arrangements for managing CRO competence, job aids for identifying CRO competencies, as well as example CRO competencies (and methods for training and assessment of those competencies) for routine, infrequent, abnormal and routine operations.

The information contained in this publication is provided for general information purposes only. Whilst the EI and the contributors have applied reasonable care in developing this publication, no warranties, express or implied, are made by the EI or any of the contributors concerning the applicability, suitability, accuracy or completeness of the information contained herein and the EI and the contributors accept no responsibility whatsoever for the use of this information. Neither the EI nor any of the contributors shall be liable in any way for any liability, loss, cost or damage incurred as a result of the receipt or use of the information contained herein.

Suggested revisions are invited and should be submitted through the Technical Department, Energy Institute, 61 New Cavendish Street, London, W1G 7AR. E: technical@energyinst.org

ACKNOWLEDGMENTS

EI *Guidance on ensuring control room operator (CRO) competence* was developed by Michael Wright, Paul Leach and Rebecca Canham of Greenstreet Berman Ltd. at the request of the EI Human and Organisational Factors Committee (HOFCOM). During this project, HOFCOM members consisted of:

John Burnett	RWE
Rebecca Ellis	EDF
Bill Gall	Kingsley Management Ltd.
Zoila Harvie	Dana Petroleum
Peter Jefferies	Phillips 66 (Vice-Chair)
Stuart King	EI
Eryl Marsh	Health and Safety Executive
Kathryn Mearns	ConocoPhillips
Rob Miles	Consultant
Allen Ormond	ABB
Graham Reeves	BP Plc. (Chair)
Helen Rycraft	International Atomic Energy Agency
Jonathan Ryder	ExxonMobil Corporation
Rob Saunders	Shell International
Gillian Vaughan	EDF
Mark Wilson	ConocoPhillips
Razif Yusoff	Shell International

Management of the project and technical editing were carried out by Stuart King (EI).

The EI acknowledges the following individuals for contributing to this project, through attendance at a stakeholder review workshop held 16 July 2013, or by reviewing the draft publication:

Rob Sutton	BP
Joanne Bailey	BP
Darren Dawson	BP
Emeke Osaje	BP
Garry Krebs	Centrica
Duncan Procter	Centrica
Tony Gower-Jones	Centrica
Dr Mark Scanlon	Energy Institute
Christopher Abraham	ExxonMobil
Craig Pugh	ExxonMobil
Paul Vowell	ExxonMobil
John Armstrong	GDF Suez
Morgan Allen	Murphy Oil
Dave Smith	Murphy Oil
Bill Goad	National Grid
Geoff Taylor	National Grid
Abrar Bajwa	National Grid
John Everett	Scotia Gas Networks
Steve Catling	Scotia Gas Networks
Andrew Barlow	Scottish and Southern Energy
Kat Feather	Shell International

Allan Greensmith   Total Lindsey Oil Refinery
Dave Jackson   Total Lindsey Oil Refinery
Peter Davidson   UKPIA

Affiliations correct at the time of contribution.

1   INTRODUCTION

1.1   SCOPE

This guide was developed to help address specific challenges relating to the competence management of control room operators (CROs). The guide is focused on the challenges (described in 2.4), identified by industry through a user requirements workshop held 16 July 2013 in London, and aims to help organisations:
–   anticipate the need for CROs when selecting the personnel from which future CROs will be selected;
–   correctly determine the competencies CROs require to help prevent major accident hazards;
–   train CROs in the right competencies;
–   ensure a robust competence assurance system for CROs is in place; and
–   strengthen organisational arrangements to support and retain CROs.

The guide covers routine, infrequent, abnormal and emergency response tasks, is focused on optimising and assuring CRO competence and briefly covers arrangements such as procedures, supervision, and control room design that support CRO performance. Case study examples, taken from a range of major hazard industries, and sources of further reading, are also provided.

1.2   WHO IS THIS GUIDE FOR?

This guide is for everyone who has responsibility for ensuring the competence of control room operators. Table 1 details which sections of the guide are most relevant for various occupational roles.

The guide has been developed for organisations operating in the energy industry, both onshore and offshore, and applies to both new and existing installations.

Table 1: Sections of guidance most relevant to various occupational roles

Occupational role	Sections of relevance
Managers and supervisors of CROs	2: Setting the scene 3: Stages of CRO development 4: Determine CRO competence requirements 6: Assess CROs 7: Retain and support CROs
Relevant members of training, human resources, learning and development, talent management functions, for example, responsible for CRO training and assessment	2: Setting the scene 3: Stages of CRO development 4: Determine CRO competence requirements 5: Train CROs 6: Assess CROs
Relevant members of health, safety, environment and quality (HSEQ) who influence and/or monitor CRO operations	2: Setting the scene 7: Retain and support CROs 8: Monitor and review CRO competence management arrangements
Internal auditors responsible for auditing CRO competence and/or competence management arrangements	2: Setting the scene 8: Monitor and review CRO competence management arrangements
Directors and senior managers responsible for safety management systems and safety cases	All sections of this guide will be of interest

2 SETTING THE SCENE

2.1 WHO IS THE CRO?

The CRO is at the heart of operations and is the key human element in the process control system. The CRO is the individual interfacing with the plant within the control room, who has direct responsibility (hands-on control) for control room operations. This includes main control rooms, satellite/remote control rooms, local control rooms and field control stations, whether in new or existing installations.

CROs can also include:
– Supervisors, who as part of their role have direct responsibility for controlling operations from the control room.
– Field operators, who may need to be familiar with control room operations, in case the main control room is disabled and there is a requirement for them to operate local/remote control rooms.
– Temporary and permanent control room operators. Staffing levels and the roles and responsibilities of CROs vary by site, meaning that permanent control room operators may not always be in place.

2.2 WHAT IS COMPETENCE MANAGEMENT?

2.2.1 Competence

Competence can be defined as 'the ability to undertake responsibilities and perform activities to a relevant standard, as necessary to ensure process safety and prevent major accidents. Competence is a combination of knowledge, skills and experience and requires a willingness and reliability that work activities will be undertaken in accordance with agreed standards, rules and procedures' (HSE, *COMAH Competent Authority, Inspection of competence management systems at COMAH establishments. Operational delivery guide*).

Competence is commonly broken down into three aspects (RSSB, *Good practice guide on competence development*):
– Knowledge: the underpinning knowledge that a CRO requires to be able to effectively carry out control room operator tasks. This might include knowledge of:
  – control room systems;
  – production processes and chemical reactions, and
  – engineering systems, safe guides and operating procedures, etc.
– Technical skills: the functional skills required to complete control room operator tasks. This might include:
  – physical operation of control room controls and devices to access system status information and relevant schematics, and
  – writing permits to work and recording relevant control room operational information during shift, handover and administration.
– Non-technical skills: the cognitive and behavioural skills required to complete control room operator tasks. This might include:
  – prioritisation of control room process information and decision making during completion of routine control room tasks;
  – communication and teamwork, and
  – willingness to respond to emergencies.

2.2.2 Competence management

Competence management can be defined as 'arrangements to control, in a logical and integrated manner, a cycle of activities within the organisation that will assure, and develop, competent performance. The aim is to ensure that individuals are clear about the performance that is expected of them, that they have received appropriate training, development and assessment, and that they maintain, or develop, their competence over time' (HSE, *COMAH Competent Authority, Inspection of competence management systems at COMAH establishments. Operational delivery guide*). Typical models and approaches to competence management can be found in Annex A.

2.3   WHY DO WE NEED COMPETENT CROs?

Competent CROs provide a number of benefits:
- **Process safety and operational efficiency**
  Competent CROs have improved diagnostic accuracy, speed and process control operation (Kluge and Burkolter, 2008). For example, '86 % of process automation professionals indicated operators had a significant impact on quality, while 78 % felt they had a significant impact on the economic performance of the plant' (Larson, 2012).
- **Cost savings**
  Effective training can help reduce plant damage, increase plant availability and reduce training costs. This is estimated at roughly $4,500 per megawatt of generating capacity per year by the Electric Power Research Institute (Ibid.).
- **Compliance improvements**
  Competent CROs have greater knowledge of process safety risks, procedures and why they need to be followed. This means they are more likely to support and comply with them.
- **Increased participation in safety**
  Increased competence and understanding of process and risk means that individuals start to take greater responsibility for safety, increasing participation in safety initiatives.

2.4   CHALLENGES ENSURING THE COMPETENCE OF CROs

A key challenge for an organisation is how to recruit and retain competent CROs in a timely and cost effective manner. Ensuring the competence of CROs starts when recruiting the operators (from whom CROs may be subsequently selected), proceeds via their training and assessment, and continues throughout their time in post.

Annex C provides self-assessment checklists to help the organisation assess how well these challenges are currently being managed.

2.4.1   Having a suitable pool of candidates

CROs are often selected from field operators. However, field operators may be recruited on the basis of their ability to be field operators rather than anticipating their future potential to be CROs. This can impact the availability of suitable CRO candidates. The challenge for organisations is how to cater for the need for CROs when recruiting field operators.

2.4.2 Using CRO standards

The CRO skill set is a combination of generic and plant specific skills and knowledge. The challenge for organisations is how to build on industry CRO standards and training to develop both generic and site-specific CRO skills and knowledge.

2.4.3 Developing potential CROs

Due to the diverse range of tasks and skills required to be a CRO, it can take a long time to train a potential CRO to full competence. This process can also be costly if the initial assessment of a candidate's potential is inadequate and subsequent training does not develop the right competencies. The process should also ensure that potential CROs are not fast-tracked too quickly.

2.4.4 Training, assessment and assurance of CRO competence

CROs' workload and shift patterns mean organisations should optimise different training approaches to train and assess competence. This optimisation relies on the competence of the trainers and assessors. The challenge for any organisation is how to ensure CROs, trainers and assessors acquire the right competencies and can demonstrate these over time.

2.4.5 Retention of CROs

Retention of CROs can also be a significant and costly challenge, as talented CROs may be tempted to move to other organisations. CROs should be provided with incentives to remain in post. This guide focuses on competence issues, such as how to enable further career development of CROs once in post.

2.4.6 Supporting CRO competence and responding to change

Organisations should have appropriate organisational arrangements to help support and retain CROs as well as manage knowledge that can be lost when CROs move roles. Practical procedures, an ergonomic work environment and supportive supervision are all part of the challenge. Organisations should also understand the impact change can have on CRO competence requirements, and review such requirements, when change occurs.

2.5 HOW DOES THIS GUIDE HELP TO ADDRESS THESE CHALLENGES?

This guide is structured around the competence management model illustrated in Figure 1 and adopts a CRO life cycle perspective, starting from ensuring a pool of CRO candidates exists, as outlined in section 3. This structure has been chosen because it:
a)   Illustrates success factors for managing CRO competence that help address the challenges identified by industry.
b)   Follows a logical approach, starting with understanding CRO competence requirements, training and assessing CROs, through to retaining and supporting CROs once in post.
c)   Aligns to a number of common approaches to competence management that are relevant to petroleum and allied industries, such as:

- HSE, *COMAH Competent Authority, Inspection of competence management systems at COMAH establishments. Operational delivery guide;*
- Cogent / UKPIA, *Guidelines for competency management systems for downstream and petroleum sites;*
- EI *Guidance on meeting expectations of EI Process safety management framework Element 3: Employee selection, placement and competency, and health assurance,* and
- CRR 348/2001 *Assessing the safety of staffing arrangements for process operations in the chemical and allied industries.*

Additional models of competence management are referenced in Annex A. A description of the model's five elements is provided in Table 2.

Within sections 4 – 6, the guide aligns training and assessment to stages in the CRO life cycle.

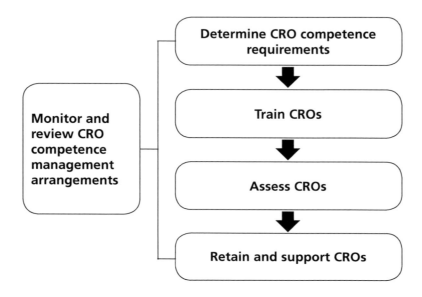

Figure 1: CRO competence management model

Table 2: Description of the CRO competence management model elements

Element	Description
Determine CRO competence requirements (section 4)	This element focuses on identifying the right knowledge, technical and non-technical skills for CROs, matched and prioritised according to major hazard risk and the development stages of CROs. This includes building upon CRO standards and regulations.
Train CROs (section 5)	This element focuses on approaches that can be used to train CROs, including linking training approaches to development stages, psychological principles for adult learning and trainer competence.

Table 2: Description of the CRO competence management model elements (continued)

Element	Description
Assess CROs (section 6)	This element firstly focuses on the assessment of underpinning skills and attitudes requisite for becoming a CRO and commencing training. Secondly, the element focuses on approaches to assess beginner- to advanced- CROs and includes assessor competence.
Retain and support CROs (section 7)	This element focuses on how organisations can enhance retention through supporting CROs.
Monitor and review CRO competence management arrangements (section 8)	This element focuses on approaches and evidence that can be used to monitor and review CRO competence arrangements.

3 STAGES OF CRO DEVELOPMENT

3.1 A DEVELOPMENT LADDER

As people do not become established CROs immediately upon selection, a progressive set of development stages can be applied. A development ladder (Figure 2) illustrates different development stages and example competencies that can be developed at each stage (Buckley and Caple, 2004):

- **'Beginner'** refers to a field operator (for example), who is developing knowledge of control room operations whilst still working as a field operator.
- **'Developing'** refers to an advanced field operator (for example), who has developed the knowledge, technical and non-technical skill to be able to take control of routine operations under supervision.
- **'Established'** refers to a qualified CRO, who can take responsibility for all control room operations independently.
- **'Advanced'** refers to a qualified CRO who has developed technical and non-technical skills to carry out some supervision duties. This stage has been included to highlight how development can be continued after the individual has been selected for the role of CRO.

To provide a structured approach to competence development, the competence requirements for each development stage should be determined, with training and assessments mapped to these development stages. This can help to assure CROs have obtained and can continually demonstrate the necessary knowledge, technical and non-technical skills required to undertake their duties competently and safely.

Guidance on: determining the competence requirements for each development stage can be found in section 4; mapping training approaches to development stages can be found in section 5; and mapping assessment approaches to development stages can be found in section 6.

Level	Description	Example competencies
Advanced	Qualified CRO with knowledge, technical and non-technical skills to undertake supervision duties and lead a small team of CROs as well as carry out expected CRO duties.	Planning and allocating work for the team and monitoring the team's performance. Coordinating emergencies and making risk based decisions under abnormal and emergency response conditions. Ensuring and challenging compliance procedures.
Established	Qualified CRO with knowledge, technical and non-technical skills developed to take responsibility for all control room operations independently.	Monitoring and maintaining health, environment and safety management systems relating to control operations, coordinating handovers and maintaining relationships with site personnel. Maintaining state of readiness and controlling critical situations, responding to emergencies including detection, diagnosis, communications and evacuations.
Developing	Advanced field operator, with technical and non-technical skills developed to take responsibility for routine control room operations and support other modes of operation (under supervision).	Accessing and interpreting equipment and system status, including detection of process upsets and understanding process to restore operations. Unit-wide knowledge including knowledge of emergency systems e.g. plant flare/vent systems, their operation and implication. Communications with site personnel, and situational awareness in routine operations.
Beginner	Field operator, with knowledge developed to understand control room operations and plant functioning. Not allowed to carry out duties in control room.	Knowledge of plant operating capacity, safe operating limits/envelope and composition of plant product properties. Knowledge of operating instructions and risks they control and ability to interpret basic control room information.

Figure 2: Development ladder

3.2 CASE STUDIES

Case study 1: CRO apprenticeship scheme

A large oil and gas company runs a CRO apprenticeship scheme. This has 15 units to be passed, that are linked to a set of development 'milestones'. The scheme lasts three years and utilises a range of training methods. This includes classroom training providing basic engineering principles, operating instructions and other safety management information, job rotation outside the control room to help individuals understand plant processes, and the effect control room operations have on these processes and safe systems of work. On-the-job training and job rotation within the control room is also provided so individuals understand and develop the competencies to undertake different tasks and roles within the control room.

Simulator training and desktop exercises are also used to help CROs develop and practise the skills required to respond to abnormal and emergency conditions.

Case study 2: 'Pipeline' talent management process

A large nuclear facility has developed a talent management process called 'Pipeline'. The aim of the process is to take beginner recruits and train them into established CROs and then up to Shift Manager. Development milestones through Pipeline have been created, with competencies detailed that must be acquired and demonstrated to achieve that milestone. A set of training modules are delivered for each milestone. Desktop exercises are used to support training and form the basis for assessments. Individuals progress to the next milestone only after all relevant training is undertaken and assessments passed.

Case study 3: Module training for new starters

A rail company has implemented a 12-month module based training programme to help CROs progress from beginner to established. The programme has modules that are focused on the development and application of knowledge and skills such as operation capacity, operating instructions and procedures, emergency procedures, alarm response and management, functional skills and relevant mandatory industry training and health and safety training.

Another set of modules are focused on non-technical skills such as communication, situational awareness, decision making, interpretation, diagnosis and assimilation of information, time management and interpersonal skills. A final set of modules is focused on basic line management, such as enforcing procedures, human factors training, coaching and project management.

4 DETERMINE CRO COMPETENCE REQUIREMENTS

A validated specification of CRO competencies, linked to the stages of development (beginner to advanced), should underpin all elements of CRO competence management. It can inform the assessment of potential CROs (see 6.1), directs the content of training (see section 5) and assessment (see 6.2) and further in-post development of CROs (see section 7). In this way, determining CRO competencies is a prerequisite for all aspects of CRO competence management.

This section focuses on helping to ensure the right knowledge, technical and non-technical skills are identified for CROs. It covers:
– how to determine critical tasks;
– approaches to identifying CRO competencies;
– developing measurable standards of performance, and
– using national and international standards and regulations.

4.1 DETERMINE CRITICAL TASKS

Critical tasks can be defined as 'Those [tasks] that have the potential, if not undertaken correctly, to initiate, propagate or exacerbate a major accident' (HSE, *COMAH Competent Authority, Inspection of competence management systems at COMAH establishments. Operational delivery guide*). Critical tasks should be identified for:
– **Normal operations**
   Critical tasks that are carried out by the CRO frequently, often on a day-to-day basis, under normal operating conditions. This might include: operating the control room under normal conditions; monitoring process and product flows; administration; issuing permits to work and communication with people inside and outside of the control room.
– **Infrequent operations**
   Critical tasks that are carried out occasionally by the CRO. In some cases CROs may not have had the opportunity to carry out these tasks within a live operating environment, but would be expected to complete them if required. Examples might include: coordinating plant shut-down and start-up; isolation of critical equipment and components for testing; initiating shut-downs and start-ups of critical assets and equipment.
– **Abnormal conditions**
   Conditions that are outside of normal/expected operating parameters, such as a potential loss of process control or a failure of equipment or monitoring systems. Abnormal condition tasks might include: using supervisory control and data acquisition (SCADA) displays to identify faults; initiation of relevant alarms; computerised operation of values to manage product flow.
– **Emergency situations**
   Any situation where there is a significant threat to life, environment, and/or plant/equipment. This may include a significant loss of process control and/or fire or gas release. Critical tasks during emergency response might include: identifying and diagnosing critical conditions; activating relevant alarms; reporting critical situations; initiating emergency procedures, including isolations, fail safes and shut-down; coordinating between people and critical communications.

For each of these, it may also be helpful to consider:
- the process/operation being undertaken, such as batch or continuous operations;
- any relevant supervision/team leader duties that may be critical for the control of major accident hazards, and
- the complexity of tasks and how often they are performed.

EI *Guidance on human factors safety critical task analysis* can be used to help determine CRO critical tasks.

Once the critical tasks have been identified, they should be validated. For example, task analyses can be compared to risk assessments described within the safety case to ensure all relevant major accident hazards and associated CRO tasks have been considered and identified.

4.2   IDENTIFY CRO COMPETENCIES

CRO critical tasks should be analysed to identify the relevant knowledge, technical and non-technical skills required to carry out the tasks reliably and safely. These can then be used as technical and/or non-technical 'markers'[1] for CRO competence assessments.

To help analyse the tasks, the following should be considered:
1. Does the task require generic and/or plant-specific knowledge and skill? For example:
   - Generic knowledge of plant operations and chemical processes, basic engineering, knowledge of complex plant, HSE regulations for COMAH sites etc.
   - Site-specific knowledge of plant layout and connective systems, process control functions, etc.
   - Specific task type knowledge, for example, testing of fire and gas control systems, diagnosis and drill down of schematics during upset conditions.
2. What technical knowledge and skills are required to undertake the task? For example:
   - Knowledge and operation of critical systems, for example, plant flare/vent systems, plant blow-down systems.
   - Understanding the limitations of these systems.
   - Knowledge of plant operating capacity, limits and composition of plant product properties.
3. What non-technical skills are required? For example:
   - Interpreting information on equipment and system status.
   - Communications during handover.
   - Prioritisation and navigation of information.

Job analysis techniques can be used to support this analysis (Doyle, 2003). These techniques should be supported by:
- Information gathered from reviewing relevant procedures.
- Observations and structured talk/walk-throughs of CROs carrying out tasks within the control room or within a simulation/simulated scenario.
- Review of safety case risk assessments and major accident scenarios. This can help ensure all relevant technical and non-technical skills and knowledge have been accurately identified.

---

1   Markers are examples of skills, knowledge, attitudes and behaviours that are required of people.

Annex D provides job aids to help identify core CRO competencies. Annexes E, F, G and H provide example generic knowledge and skills for routine, infrequent, abnormal and emergency tasks, along with training and assessment methods.

4.2.1 Map competencies to CRO development stages

Whilst a common set of competencies might be determined, the type of competencies to develop and assess may vary across the development stages. For example:
–   Beginner CRO competencies may focus on underpinning knowledge requirements, i.e. understanding the plant, role of control room operations and the CRO, rather than the skills required to handle routine operations.
–   Developing CRO competencies may additionally focus on the technical and non-technical skills required to handle routine operations, under supervision.
–   Established CRO competencies may additionally focus on the technical and non-technical skills to handle infrequent, abnormal and emergency operations, without requiring supervisor guidance.
–   Advanced CRO competencies may additionally cover the technical and non-technical skills required to supervise CROs, manage complex infrequent activities such as shut-downs, plan complex work schedules and potentially train and assess CRO competence.

All CRO competencies should be determined first and then segmented and defined per CRO development stage. Once all relevant knowledge, technical and non-technical skills have been defined, they can be prioritised to help inform the frequency and depth of training and assessment required. This may be done by asking CROs, their supervisors and other relevant subject matter experts to rank the importance of each knowledge and skill for successful task completion.

4.3   CREATE MEASURABLE PERFORMANCE STATEMENTS/STANDARDS

Measurable standards of performance describe 'competent' CRO performance for each critical task. They can be used as learning objectives for CRO training and criteria for CRO competence assessments (HSE, *Competence assessment for the hazardous industries*). They should reflect the competencies required for each development stage; example measurable statements are given in Table 3.

Table 3: Example measurable competence performance standards

Stage	Example measurable statement
Beginner	Beginner CROs must be able to successfully describe the operating capacity of the plant and the main functions of the control room.
Developing	Developing CROs must be able to successfully access and interpret routine SCADA information, determining and describing current system status.
Established	Established CROs must be able to describe how the fire and gas control system works, be able to detect and interpret the alarms associated with the system and carry out expected control room actions as described in company procedures.

Table 3: Example measurable competence performance standards (continued)

Stage	Example measurable statement
Advanced	Advanced CROs must be able to manage the completion of infrequent operations, such as removing and replacing a hydrocarbon pump, starting from developing the plan of working, specifying permits to work, instructing relevant staff and monitoring relevant control room instrumentation to understand pump integrity and stability before start-up.

Statements should be measurable, in that it is possible to identify a way of either observing the person performing the actions correctly and/or they can verbally state the required knowledge.

Standards often describe the minimum level of competence needed to carry out critical roles. If possible, measurable statements of performance should describe 'competent', 'expert' and 'proficient' performance (RSSB, *Good practice guide on competence development*). This may help to create a culture of learning, and communicates to CROs that the organisation wishes to help CROs strive for excellence.

4.3.1 Utilise national and international standards and regulations

National and international standards and regulations, for example National Occupational Standards (NOSs) and the aforementioned HSE *Inspection of competence management systems at COMAH Establishments*, can be used to help determine CRO competence requirements, creating measurable statements of performance. However, as these are generic, it may be helpful to map site- and plant-specific CRO competencies onto these standards/regulations and identify any gaps.

Table 4 describes three steps that can be followed.

Table 4: Steps to map plant-specific CRO competencies

Steps	Guidance
Step 1: Gap analysis	Compare the CRO activities, requirements, knowledge and skills described in the standard and/or regulation against your identified CRO competence requirements. From this determine: 1. Relevance – Is the standard and/or regulation relevant? Are all areas relevant, or certain parts? Do existing CRO competence frameworks and/or training and assessment programmes already cover the content? 2. Removals – Can areas be removed if they are not relevant? (e.g. modules of a training programme). 3. Additions – Do additional modules/elements need to be created or existing ones revised to meet competence requirements?

Table 4: Steps to map plant-specific CRO competencies (continued)

Steps	Guidance
Step 2: Populate	Based on the gap analysis: 1. Remove, if possible, areas that are irrelevant. 2. Work through each relevant module/element outlined and describe CRO knowledge, technical and non-technical skills that relate to that module/element. Use short, clear statements. 3. Create additional modules/elements. For example, with a National Vocation Qualification (NVQ), additional training modules could be created. When amending and/or creating additional areas, the following should be described: the type of task the CRO will be undertaking (routine, infrequent, abnormal, emergency); the critical tasks the relevant knowledge, technical and non-technical skills required, and grouped (where applicable) per CRO development stage.
Step 3: Review and validate	Where amendments or additional modules have been developed it may be useful to have them reviewed before being implemented. CROs and their supervisors/managers can be asked to review amendments and/or additional modules.

Once reviewed, validated and accepted, it should be planned how the standard and/or relegation will be implemented across the organisation. Table 5 describes a number of areas to consider.

Table 5: Considerations for implementing standards and/or regulations

Areas to consider	Guidance
How will standards/ regulations be implemented?	1. Determine how the standard and/or regulation can be incorporated into existing training and assessment programmes, for example: – Can an NVQ or National Skills Academy training course be incorporated into existing talent management arrangements or current CRO training and assessment? – Can a new standard or regulation be turned into an additional training module and incorporated into ongoing CRO training and assessment? – Can existing CRO training and assessment be adjusted to take account of new standards, regulations and any additions developed? 2. Consider the range of training and assessment methods available for implementation (on-the-job, peer assisted, self-directed and simulations) to help reduce the potential workload burden on CROs, trainers and assessors. 3. Identify any additional competencies the trainers and assessors require.

Table 5: Considerations for implementing standards and/or regulations (continued)

Areas to consider	Guidance
What will be the ongoing training and assessment requirements?	1. Determine the type and frequency of ongoing training and assessment. This should be informed by criticality of the CRO tasks, the frequency CRO tasks are performed, and likely degradation of competence over time.
How will the implementation be communicated?	1. Line manager/CRO pre-implementation discussions should take place, covering purpose of the standards and/regulations, benefits it will bring the CRO and the business, activities the CRO will be undertaking, timescales for implementation, work demands etc, and support the CRO will receive from the line manager, colleagues and the business. 2. Follow-up discussions should take place throughout implementation (if applicable) to identify any barriers to demonstrating competence and further competence needs. 3. Post-implementation discussions should set out ongoing mentoring and development activities and schedule (if possible and relevant) of ongoing assessments.
How will the implementation be reviewed?	1. Review once implemented. If possible, such as with NVQs, the review can be undertaken throughout the programme to determine whether it is developing the right competencies. 2. Ideally use a combination of CRO feedback, CRO competence assessment and re-assessment, CRO job performance data and reported process upsets, near misses, incidents, accidents etc. related to control room operations and the competence of CROs. 3. The review should help determine if the standard and/or regulation has met CRO competence needs and what improvements can be made.

Annex D provides a job aid to help the organisation make use of relevant standards.

4.4 DEVEOP CRO TASK INVENTORIES

CRO competence requirements can be collated into CRO task inventories, per CRO development stage, and ideally (and where applicable) per operational condition, i.e. normal operations, infrequent tasks, plant upset/abnormal conditions and emergency situations.

An example way of structuring a CRO task inventory for an 'established' CRO, using an example abnormal condition task, is provided in Table 6. CRO task inventories should also contain information on CRO training and assessment requirements. Sections 5 and 6 provide guidance to help determine this information.

Table 6: Established CRO task inventory for abnormal operations (example task)

Critical tasks	Knowledge	Technical skills	Non-technical skill	Statement of competent performance	Training required	Assessments required
Initiating emergency procedures due to leak of hydrocarbon from a storage tank	Knowledge of hazards and operating rules and limits	Physical activation of relevant isolation controls	Information acquisition and assimilation Ability to control stress levels	Individual demonstrates ability to come to a timely decision about emergency response actions Individual remains calm and composed throughout event	Interactive classroom training on knowledge of hazards, operating rules and limits, processes Structured scenario learning, taking individual through each element of emergency management for this event	Verbal or written knowledge assessment covering knowledge of hazards, operating rules, limits, processes Simulated exercise assessing the individual's skills to carry out emergency response management

4.5   CASE STUDIES

Case study 4: Critical tasks and competencies for upset condition and emergency response tasks

A multi-national gas company used critical task analysis and critical incident techniques to identify the competencies required to complete upset condition tasks and emergency response tasks.

Procedures were reviewed, with task analysis used to identify the critical tasks to be completed. Scenario based walk-throughs were then conducted, along with interviews with CROs who had been involved in upset conditions and emergency responses. These were used to help validate the task analysis and start to identify the technical and non-technical skills. A review of near miss, incident and accident reports from within the company and also across the industry were used to help identify competencies, coupled with critical incident interviews with operators.

Based on this information a set of technical and non-technical markers were developed. These were validated through comparing the information to risk assessments completed as part of the safety case. They were also applied to major accident scenarios that were described within the safety case, to validate the markers. Finally operators, supervisors and subject matter specialists were asked to peer review the markers. The markers were used to identify training needs and develop a suite of technical training, non-technical training and assessments that focused on assessing both technical and non-technical knowledge and skill within a scenario/simulated environment.

Case study 5: Using CRO National Occupational Standards (NOSs) to create CRO training

An organisation refining and distributing petroleum used CRO NOSs to create an accredited CRO training programme. The programme awards CROs with an NVQ and then a Foundation Degree. The NOSs were populated with plant/terminal-specific CRO technical and non-technical knowledge and skills. Additional elements were added relating to emergency response procedures, local safe systems of work and specific process controls, roles and operations expected in the control room.

NOSs were collated into a CRO competence framework (meeting Cogent industry-endorsed *Gold standard* competency framework for the process industries). The training programme was structured around each element of the framework. The programme utilises formal training, on-the-job training, and self-directed continuing professional development (CPD), with ongoing assesments matched to task frequency and criticality and role-specfic abilities. Trainers and assessors are provided with train the trainer sessions to ensure competence.

The programme is audited externally and internally to understand whether the competence framework is up to date and accurate and if the training is effective.

---

5   TRAIN CROs

Suitable and effective training, matched to the appropriate stage of development (for example beginner to advanced), can allow CROs to develop the necessary knowledge, technical and non-technical skills required to undertake their role.

This section focuses on providing suitable and effective training to CROs. It covers:
– identifying training needs;
– mapping training approaches to CRO development stages, and
– creating a positive learning environment.

The content and form of training may match the competencies defined per CRO stage, such as:
– introductory training for beginner CROs;
– in-depth training for developing CROs;
– refresher training for established CROs, and
– specialist training for advanced CROs.

The form of training is also likely to be determined by the type of knowledge and skill, task frequency and task difficulty.

It should be noted that a developing CRO may be trained in the competencies for an established CRO once they have been assessed as satisfying the criteria for a developing CRO. Once a person is an established CRO they may need refresher training, especially for infrequent, abnormal and emergency tasks.

Annexes E, F, G and H provide example methods for training CROs for routine, infrequent, abnormal and emergency operations.

5.1   IDENTIFY TRAINING NEEDS

To develop and maintain the skills and knowledge of CROs, training needs should be identified (RSSB, *Risk based training needs analysis. Guide to the process and templates*). This includes mandatory training and qualifications relevant to the tasks, and skills and knowledge needed to complete those tasks.

To help identify CRO training needs, the following should be considered:
– Frequency of performance – how often is the task performed and is the execution of the task observable? e.g. manual tasks vs. decision making.
– Difficulty of task – how difficult is the task to learn and perform competently?
– Skill vs. knowledge – are skills, knowledge, or both being developed?
– Generic vs. site/plant-specific – are generic and/or plant/site-specific knowledge and skill being developed?
– Development stage – what type and duration of experience is required for each stage? For example, a developing CRO may be required to undertake six months' supervised operation of critical routine tasks before being allowed to carry out these tasks independently.
– Current assessments – if applicable, what training needs have been identified from previous competence assessments?

This information may help to determine:

- Type of training, for example: classroom based, on-the-job and/or scenario learning.
- Level/depth of training, for example: a briefing, one-day session or a set of detailed modules.
- Content of training, for example: technical knowledge and/or skill development.
- Type and frequency of refresher training, for example: no refresher training as task is performed daily and is of low difficulty; or on-the-job refresher training every three years, as task is performed regularly and is of medium difficulty; or yearly scenario based refresher training as task is performed infrequently and is difficult to perform.
- Assessment requirements, for example: type, frequency and structure of assessments.
- Trainer/assessor competence, for example: technical understanding of chemical processes and engineering, non-technical skills such as coaching, observation and providing constructive feedback.

5.2   MAP TRAINING TO DEVELOPMENT STAGES

Mapping training to CRO development stages may help develop the correct competencies for each stage (Berger and Berger, 2011). As part of this, relevant qualifications required for each development stage should be identified.

To help CROs progress through the development stages it can be useful to maximise training methods that expose CROs to a range of plant and control room operations. A good way to do this is through modular training, using approaches like on-the-job training, shadowing, observations, scenario exercises and job rotation. These approaches help maximise CRO exposure to plant and control room operations.

Table 7 illustrates example training for the development stages.

Table 7: Example training approaches mapped to development stages

Development stage	Example training
Beginner	- Job rotation of selected field operator roles to develop knowledge of plant operations and activities. On-the-job training structured around developing understanding of how control room operations affect plant operation. - Classroom training focusing on technical understanding of operating instructions. Supported by facilitated scenarios, simulators or simulation of routine operations. Structured self-directed assignments to learn about specific plant operations and control room operations. Structured shadowing and observations of control room operations to understand the basic operations, context and information to interpret.
Developing	- Shadowing of control room operations and job rotation, with structured on-the-job training to undertake routine operations under supervision with targeted coaching. Classroom training focused on non-technical skills to undertake routine operations. Taking part in facilitated scenario-based learning (simulators or simulation) to develop these skills. Structured self-directed assignments to enhance these skills plus any mandatory training required by the organisation or regulator.

Table 7: Example training approaches mapped to development stages (continued)

Development stage	Example training
Established	To reach the 'established' stage further training may focus on: – Shadowing of infrequent tasks and process upset conditions, and job rotation to undertake duties in these conditions, if possible. Simulated or simulation of these conditions focused on allowing the CRO to take full control of operations, reducing and eventually eliminating the requirement for supervision. – Classroom training focusing on advanced non-technical skills, particularly for infrequent, abnormal and emergency response situations. This can include crew resource management (CRM) training, basic safety leadership training, safety behaviour awareness training and risk-based decision making. Also any mandatory training required by the organisation or regulator.
Advanced	– Classroom training focusing on supervision and leadership skills, basic incident command and relevant management training such as Institution of Occupational Safety and Health (IOSH) *Managing safely*. This should be supported by on-the-job training, focusing on basic supervision. – Scenario-based learning (simulators or simulation) to develop skills in coordinating emergencies and ensuring compliance. This can include shadowing supervisors during these scenarios. Job rotation, to practise allocating and monitoring a small number of tasks performed by a team of CROs. – Any mandatory training required by the organisation or regulator for supervision.

5.3 CREATE A POSITIVE LEARNING ENVIRONMENT

To help create a positive learning environment, CRO training can be designed around psychological principles for adult learning (Jarvis et al, 2003; Krause et al, 2002). These principles are summarised in Figure 3. Annex D provides a job aid detailing the principles of adult learning.

Figure 3: Psychological principles for adult learning

5.3.1 Motivation

Motivation to acquire/refresh knowledge or skills can be fostered by helping CROs understand how training and development will benefit them. To achieve this, training can be selected based on identified training needs, task criticality and the specific competencies to be developed.

Adult learners may resist learning if they feel it is being imposed on them. Fostering individual responsibility for learning may help to motivate CROs and improve the learning experience. One way of achieving this is to create graded CRO learning programmes, meaning that as the CRO moves through a programme, opportunities for self-directed learning increase and direct supervision of them decreases.

Motivation and responsibility for learning can also be fostered through developing group and individual activities requiring CROs to take concepts, theories, and information being taught and generate learning outputs that they then apply in the control room with the support of line managers and peers.

5.3.2 Experience

Experience is a source of an adult's identity. Learning material taught to CROs should be integrated into their own experiences to complement existing knowledge. For example, the frequency of refresher training should be matched to task criticality, difficulty and frequency of performance, demonstrating how training enhances or 'refreshes' CROs' existing knowledge.

CROs should also be provided with reflective learning opportunities, including peer feedback, to help them reflect on how existing knowledge and ways of working can be enhanced.

5.3.3 Learn by doing

CRO training should always involve a high level of practice and application. For example, training can present theory and concepts, and then the use of activities, scenarios, on-the-job training, etc, can provide practice, coupled with constructive feedback. These activities should be set within a context that a CRO can relate to, with a focus on helping them tackle/ solve problems that they commonly face. Table 8 describes some key considerations when developing practical-based learning activities.

Table 8: Considerations for developing practical-based learning activities

Areas to consider	Guidance
Matching practical-based learning to specific training needs.	Identified critical tasks, competencies and measurable statements of performance can be used to structure learning activities as they describe the types of tasks, behaviours, skills, knowledge and performance the CRO is expected to demonstrate during activities.
Covering the range of task types (routine, infrequent, abnormal and emergency response).	Practical-based learning should look to develop both knowledge and skill, either technical and/or non-technical across the activities. As part of this, it is helpful to identify whether the application of the skill/ knowledge can be observed within an activity or whether it will need to be explained/talked through by the CRO.
Making activities realistic and safe.	Any activity/scenario should match task characteristics and operational mode, and provide a safe learning environment. For example, abnormal and emergency response CRO tasks should be mocked-up using dynamic and changing scenarios or desktop activities, whereas routine tasks can more easily be trained within a control room environment using structured on-the-job training.

CROs may also learn better in an informal environment, meaning training opportunities that do not require the CRO to sit in a classroom should be maximised. Adults also like variety in teaching, so it is beneficial to use different training methods. This is sometimes termed 'blended learning' (see Kluge and Burkolter, 2010; IAEA-TECDOC-1411; Kim and Byun, 2011), utilising methods such as multimedia materials, interactive discovery activities, role-plays, mock-ups, case studies, simulations, on-the-job and peer-led teaching, and self-directed and e-learning.

5.3.4 Respect and trust

Adults learn better if they are respected and they trust the trainer (i.e. are confident that the trainer has the necessary skills, knowledge and experience). Respect can be demonstrated through effective facilitation, such as taking an interest in CROs' questions, thoughts and feedback, acknowledging experiences of CROs and the level of experience they have. It is also important to encourage CROs to express ideas, reasoning, thoughts and decisions.

Trainer competence should be developed in the same way as CROs, using job analysis techniques, developing measurable standards of performance, providing relevant training and assessments. The frequency, level and depth of training and assessment should be matched to:
–   the type of trainer skills and knowledge required;
–   the safety criticality of the topic/CRO tasks being trained;
–   how often the trainer delivers the training, and
–   complexity of the topic being taught.

Annex I provides example competencies of trainers, and methods for training and assessing trainer competence.

5.3.5   Feedback

CROs require constructive feedback during any form of training. Feedback should be:
–   Specific, to help improvement.
–   Objective and evidence based.
–   Motivating and focused on strengths and areas of development.
–   Structured around technical and non-technical markers, which are derived from the CRO measurable statements.
–   Provided in different forms, for example, face-to-face, development reports, self-evaluation questionnaires, activities and scenarios with feedback by both trainers and peers.

5.4   CASE STUDIES

Case study 6: CRM training

Nuclear power plants used CRM training to help develop the skills of the CROs, focusing on six multiple fault scenarios that required the CRO to carry out a range of mitigation activities and communicate and coordinate with personnel within and outside the control room. Training specialists acted as the personnel within and outside the control room, providing critical communications when required, in line with the different scenarios.

A safety culture and attitudinal assessment was carried out to help develop the CRM training, by identifying the types of skills that needed to be developed within the simulator. This included leadership, task management, communication, risk management, situational awareness, decision making and self management.

Behavioural markers were developed for each which helped to structure the training, the feedback provided to operators and the eventual assessment of competence.

The simulator practice was supported by classroom based teaching, which focused on developing the non-technical knowledge of CROs, helping them to understand the underpinning principles of each skill being developed and how they help the CRO to perform efficiently, safely and support the control of major accident hazards.

The training also utilised 'peer facilitators'. These are advanced CROs who are taken off operational duties to help teach the CROs, explaining how the non-technical skills help them in their role and how to apply these skills within the control room.

Case study 7: Simulation of critical emergency response systems

A multinational oil and gas company simulates the activation of critical emergency response systems such as electrostatic discharge (EDS) and fire and gas control systems. A range of different fault scenarios are used to simulate activation of the systems. The simulations are firstly focused on technical knowledge that is helping CROs understand what the critical systems are, what their activation consists of, the alarms that are activated and the reasons why they activate. This also covers the safeguards the systems have in place, their operating limits and tolerance and how they support the control/mitigation of major accident hazards within an emergency response.

Once CROs have developed this knowledge, the next part of the simulator training is focused on skill development in terms of: activation of relevant alarms; controls and devices; fault finding and diagnosis; the information the CRO needs to locate, interpret and monitor; critical actions, decisions and communications.

Relevant feedback and assessments take place to develop and assure competence.

Case study 8: 24 hrs simulator

A multinational oil and gas company has a CRO simulator that is accessible 24 hrs. The simulator uses dynamic modelling and provides a range of real-life scenarios and situations that are faced by the CRO, including fault scenarios, infrequent critical tasks, example incidents/accidents and example emergencies. The CRO is able to programme the simulator to 'play' the situations/scenarios to help them develop and practise their skills. The simulator also provides opportunities for assessing skills so CROs can understand how they performed during a scenario and start to determine new training needs. This style of direct learning is supported by line management and relevant CRO trainers who monitored learning, and helps the CRO reflect on performance and identify training needs.

Case study 9: Scenario based learning

A multinational oil and gas company developed scenario based non-technical skills training. A review of recent incidents and near misses, performance data and hazard spotting data was conducted to pick a selection of challenging scenarios. These covered infrequent tasks, abnormal operations and emergency response situations. Task analysis and measurable standards, described in current competence frameworks, were used to identify the types of tasks and behaviours/performance expected of CROs during the scenarios. All the scenarios were reviewed and validated by subject matter specialists to ensure that each scenario was realistic and that the tasks and behaviours/performance expected of CROs were in line with procedures and good practice.

The training consisted of theories and concepts, relating to non-technical skills such as communication, safety leadership, and risk based decision making, being presented to CROs within a classroom.

The scenarios were then used to help CROs apply and practise these skills. The scenarios consisted of simulated mock-ups within the training facility as well as picture based desktop activities. Each CRO was required to solve the situation presented to them, leading a small group of peers. After resolution of the scenario, the CROs were provided feedback on performance by the trainer and then their peers. Each CRO was given the opportunity to complete a scenario.

The difficulty and challenging nature of the scenarios increased as the training progressed.

6   ASSESS CROs

Assessment underpins the competence management process. It helps an organisation identify candidates with the potential to perform the CRO role in the future, and assure, over time, that CROs have acquired the right competencies, from beginner to advanced, and can demonstrate these on a continual basis. To support this process, assessment approaches should be mapped to the stages of development, with assessment required to allow progress from one stage to the next.

This section covers:
- approaches to assessing the underpinning skills and attitudes (i.e. potential) to become CROs in the future;
- assessing beginner to advanced CROs;
- assessor competence, and
- communicating assessment results so as to inform ongoing training and assessment.

6.1   ASSESS POTENTIAL TO BECOME BEGINNER CROs

6.1.1   Create a pool of candidates

A sufficient pool of candidates with the potential to perform the role of a CRO is a prerequisite to the success of any selection process. As many companies select CROs from existing staff, the recruitment of staff should anticipate and cater for subsequent CRO staffing needs. This also means that the impact of resourcing policies on the availability of candidates should be recognised. For example, the number of field operators should be sufficient to allow some to progress on to becoming CROs. Similarly, the impact of outsourcing functions (again using field operations as an example), compared to retaining functions in-house onsite, on being able to recruit CROs from current site staff should be considered – i.e. contracting out operational roles might restrict the pool of candidates.

To develop a candidate pool of potential CROs, at least some field operators (for example) should be recruited on the basis that they have the underpinning skills and attitudes (i.e. *Potential*) to become CROs in the future.

6.1.2   Assess candidates

To help achieve this, assessments of *Potential* can be conducted, focused on the following underpinning skills and attitudes:
1.   the critical cognitive skills that can be used to maintain situational awareness of plant functioning;
2.   the critical non-technical skills that can be applied to work effectively and safely within a control room environment, and
3.   the working style, values and beliefs that fit the culture of the organisation.

These have been shown to be good predictors of future job performance (Cook, 2004). Furthermore, as the assessment of *Potential* focuses on underlying skills and attitudes, technical knowledge does not need to be included in the assessment. Table 9 details the different methods that can be used to assess these underpinning skills and attitudes.

One of the most effective approaches to assessing *Potential* is an assessment centre (Ibid.), whether this is conducted in-house or externally. This is an evaluation process consisting of activities and tests administered over a day. It allows a large number of candidates to be assessed at one time and is often one of the best predictors of future job performance.

During assessment there should be criteria for screening out individuals who do not possess the desired level of *Potential*. The assessment methods described in Table 9 may also provide information to inform career and work placement decisions for those individuals.

Table 9: Methods to assess critical underpinning skills and attitudes

Example underpinning skills and attitudes	Example methods to assess the underlying skills and attitudes
Cognitive skills to maintain situational awareness: a) Numerical reasoning b) Verbal reasoning c) Inductive and deductive reasoning	Numerical reasoning tests Measures ability to draw correct conclusions and inferences from numerical or statistical data. Verbal reasoning tests Measures ability to evaluate the logic of various kinds of argument as presented in written form. Inductive reasoning tests Measures ability to draw inferences and understand the relationships between various concepts. Deductive reasoning tests Measures ability to draw logical conclusions based on information provided and complete scenarios using incomplete information.
Critical non-technical skills: a) Communications b) Decision making c) Team working	Situational judgement tests Assesses ability to make decisions and choose the most appropriate action in workplace situations. Work sample tests Example scenarios that have occurred within control room operations (basic operations) to assess decision making style, communications and teamwork. This can also be timed to assess decision making ability under timed conditions. Task oriented group activities Non-work related scenario to assess individual's ability to communicate and work as a team. Also tests leadership potential.

Table 9: Methods to assess critical underpinning skills and attitudes (continued)

Example underpinning skills and attitudes	Example methods to assess the underlying skills and attitudes
Cultural fit a) Preferred working style and values and match to the organisation b) Motivation c) Interests and career aspirations	Team inventories Questionnaires that measure preferred style of team working. Personality questionnaires Measures an individual's behavioural style to understand the impact this will have on working relationships, safety and performance. Motivation inventories Questionnaires to understand what motivates and de-motivates candidates. Assessment of cultural fit is often a good predictor of retention. i.e. the better the fit, the greater the chance of retaining the individual. Structured interest interview Face-to-face interview to understand personal background, interests and career aspirations.

6.2 ASSESS BEGINNER TO ADVANCED CROs

On an ongoing basis, CROs should be assessed in order to progress them up the development ladder. Annexes E, F G and H contain example methods for assessing CROs' knowledge and skills for routine, infrequent, abnormal and emergency operations.

6.2.1 Criteria for assessment

CRO task inventories, as described in 4.4, provide the information to develop assessment criteria, i.e.:
- Critical tasks – these are the tasks that CROs will be required to perform during assessments.
- Measurable statements of performance – for each critical task, these describe the level of performance CROs are expected to demonstrate during assessments.
- Knowledge, technical and non-technical skills – these are the markers to guide assessments. They describe the knowledge, technical and non-technical skills a CRO must have acquired and be able to exhibit to the level required.

Assessment criteria should be developed for each development stage covering, as applicable, routine, infrequent, abnormal and emergency response conditions.

6.2.2 Methods and evidence

A range of assessment methods can be used to ensure sufficient evidence is gathered to make accurate judgements of CRO competence. Table 10 provides guidance to help determine:
- Type of assessment: for example, observation, scenario/simulation, written test, cognitive walk-through.

- Depth of assessment, for example, focusing on the performance of one critical task, or multiple tasks and operations.
- Content of assessment, for example, assessment of technical knowledge only (written assessment) or assessing skill and knowledge (cognitive walk-through).
- Frequency of assessment, for example, annual assessments for routine tasks, biannual for emergency response tasks, or maybe an impromptu assessment, such as if a CRO made a number of errors dealing with a recent process upset condition.

Table 10: Guidance to help inform CRO competence assessment

Questions	Guidance
How critical is the task?	If it is a prioritised critical task it is likely to require rigorous and frequent assessments.
How often is the task performed?	High risk low frequency performed tasks may require increased rigour and frequency of assessment using scenario/simulator assessments. High risk high frequency tasks may require frequent on-the-job assessments focused on specific areas.
How difficult is the task to learn and perform competently?	With complex tasks there may be a greater risk of CROs forgetting certain elements, and hence a more rigorous assessment may be required to assess all aspects of the complex task.
Are skills, knowledge or both being assessed?	Knowledge assessments may require written tests or knowledge based task walk-throughs. Skill assessments may require observations of CROs carrying out tasks. For many cases it may be possible to devise assessments that assess both knowledge and skill.
What is the CRO development stage?	Beginner and developing CROs may require a range of different on-the-job assessments and mentoring to ensure they are developing the right competencies. Established and advanced CROs may require a range of staggered assessments to ensure they have maintained their competence and continue to perform to the required standard.

To support judgements of CRO competence, assessments should be mapped to CRO development stages. Table 11 illustrates some examples.

Table 11: Example assessment approaches mapped to CRO development stages

Development stage	Example assessments
Beginner	Written tests Focused on assessing different areas of knowledge. This could include a beginner CRO observing a qualified CRO carry out routine activities, with the beginner explaining to an assessor the purpose of each action. This can help to assess technical knowledge and understanding of skills required. Desktop task tests Desktop exercises using talk/walk-through assessment to test knowledge, for example, understanding the impact that control room operations have on plant.
Developing	Live tests Talk/walk-through assessment of live routine tasks being completed in the control room, focused on knowledge, technical skill and non-technical skills. This could include a developing CRO observing an established or advanced CRO carrying out routine (common) tasks, with the developing CRO explaining to an assessor the purpose of each action. Written tests To assess different areas of knowledge relating to routine tasks.
Established	Live tests Test ability to undertake critical routine operations in a live control room without supervision. This should include the candidate undertaking each task unaided and talking through why they are doing each task, the effect it will have, potential risks to safety, process control being observed and the relationship between tasks. If possible a live test should be carried out for infrequent tasks as well, such as shut-down or isolation of critical assets and/or equipment. Mock-ups/simulators or desktop task tests Test ability to undertake critical infrequent, abnormal and emergency response tasks. This should provide challenging scenarios, with multiple factors to consider in resolving the situation. Candidates should firstly be asked to resolve the situation and coordinate the response. Observations should be made of actions and skills demonstrated. Candidates should then be asked to talk through their actions, in terms of why they did each task, the effect it had, risks to safety and process being controlled, potential risks that were considered, the relationship between tasks, and additional considerations. This will help to assess technical and non-technical knowledge and skill and supervision potential.

Table 11: Example assessment approaches mapped to CRO development stages (continued)

Development stage	Example assessments
	Time-critical test These tests focus on the demonstration of critical cognitive abilities within a specific time period. These desktop tests are based on scenarios that have occurred within the plant or other similar industries and require CROs to assimilate and interpret specific information relating to an abnormal or emergency response, detecting and diagnosing faults, prioritising information, and deciding on action.
	Written test Multiple choice questions to test technical knowledge of, for example, critical systems, plant operating capacity and limits and composition of plant product properties.
Advanced	Supervision activities Mock-up scenario to assess safety leadership. Scenarios can be mocked-up to assess ability to challenge unsafe acts and non-compliances, carry out coaching sessions to tackle poor performance, and deliver engaging toolbox talks.
	Desktop exercises to assess individual's completion of typical supervision duties such as organising work schedules and shift rotas.
	These can be triangulated with a walk-through of control room activities to assess technical understanding of procedures and the risks they control. This supports ability to promote safe behaviour and procedural compliance.
	Command and control activities Simulator or simulation of emergency responses and abnormal conditions to assess potential command and control skills.
	Leadership assessment Leadership assessment questionnaires, including 360 degree feedback tools, to understand leadership potential, type of leadership style, strategic decision making style, key strengths and areas of risk.

Consider developing assessment methods that can be administered at local sites or centrally at headquarters or main operating sites. Such methods include process simulators/simulation, written tests, structured cognitive walk-throughs and work sample tests. This may help reduce assessment cost and time demand, and increase consistency of assessments. The frequency and method of assessments should also be flexible to allow for changes in equipment, working practices etc.

Any type of assessment method should be:
- Reliable – the assessment produces consistent results that are trusted by assessors, CROs and line managers.
- Valid – the assessment measures what it is supposed to measure i.e. specific measures of performance and knowledge and skills required for effective performance.
- Authentic – CROs cannot cheat the assessment and it is clear the evidence gathered from the assessment is the CRO's own work.
- Fair – the assessment does not discriminate against characteristics such as gender, age, ethnicity etc.

6.2.3 Judging competence

A judgement of competence is the extent to which a CRO has demonstrated the required level of performance for a given critical task and exhibited the desired knowledge, technical and non-technical skills to achieve that performance (Wright et al, 2003).

To reduce bias, a number of assessors can be involved in assessments. Available on-the-job performance information and feedback from supervisors and managers can also be used to help make judgements of competence.

'Pass/fail' criteria can also be used. This can be particularly useful for elements/areas of assessment that are considered 'critical', i.e. if the CRO is unable to perform a critical task correctly or give the right answer to a critical knowledge question first time, then they are automatically deemed 'not competent'.

Judgements of competence should be recorded to create a CRO competence portfolio, which can sit alongside CRO task inventories. The portfolio might include information such as:
- CRO name;
- competence profile of all competencies and tasks assessed;
- standard achieved;
- copy of certificate(s) to operate (if applicable);
- expiry date of certificates (to trigger reassessments);
- evidence for judgements of competence including:
  - dates of assessment;
  - methods of assessment;
  - name and signature of assessors;
  - assessment results;
  - deficiencies in competence, actions and reassessment undertaken (if applicable), and
- plan for ongoing development and maintenance of competence, including ongoing training and development and reassessments.

Reviewing the portfolio may help identify strengths and weaknesses of CROs and inform ongoing training. For example, assessment results may be used to select jobs for rotation or shadowing opportunities for beginner and/or developing CROs. This may help to keep assessments focused on the needs of potential CROs (Marcella et al, 2011) rather than just becoming a 'tick box' exercise.

A system should be in place for CROs deemed 'not competent', focusing on helping them reach the desired level of competence without compromising plant safety. One way to do this is to determine what type of operations and duties CROs are able to undertake if they are deemed 'not competent' and provide coaching, training and reassessment targeted towards specific areas of concern.

6.3 ASSESSOR COMPETENCE

The competence of assessors should be developed and assessed so they can accurately and reliably assess and judge CRO competence. The competence of assessors should be developed in the same way as CRO trainers (see 5.3.4).

Annex I provides example competencies assessors should have, and methods for training and assessing assessor competence.

6.4   COMMUNICATE ASSESSMENT RESULTS

Assessment results should be communicated to:
–   CROs and/or potential CROs, to help them understand their strengths and weaknesses and support their ongoing development.
–   Relevant line managers, to help them identify how they will support CROs and/or potential CROs and implement any actions required to tackle shortfalls in competence.
–   Relevant trainers, to help them identify specific training that may be required to tackle shortfalls in competence.

Finally, it can be helpful to look at assessment results across all CROs and/or potential CROs to try and identify common competence shortfalls. This information may highlight new training needs and/or provide an indication of how effective the training is.

6.5   CASE STUDIES

Case study 10: Assessing *Potential*

A large rail company uses an assessment centre to assess CRO *Potential*. The assessment centre utilises a number of different methods. This includes: verbal and numerical reasoning tests to assess cognitive ability; group activities (that are not related to the working environment) to assess communication skills, ability to influence and working within a team; and a competency based interview to explore how individuals might behave within a given operational scenario and the types of competencies they might demonstrate.

Finally a personality measure is also used. This helps to assess relevant personality traits relating to decisiveness, rule consciousness, organisation, and openness to change. This is also used to help understand the person/culture fit. For successful candidates information gathered from this initial assessment is used to identify key areas of strength and weakness and to inform ongoing training and assessment requirements.

Case study 11: Process simulator assessments

An organisation responsible for space station control centre operations uses simulator assessments to maintain competence certification of control room operators. Before the assessments take place, preparation training is provided to the operators. This includes overview of operations flow/concepts, science that underpins these operations, ground commanding, crew operations and 'what if' scenarios.

Simulations focus on three areas:
–   Communications – complex distributed communications across teams to plan activities, report system status and coordinate recovery from abnormalities.
–   Situational awareness – listen to radio conversations, understand what other team members are doing, identify how this may affect control room operations, identify and manage conflicting priorities and actions as well as maintain a clear understanding of system status and functioning.

Case study 11: Process simulator assessments (continued)

- Detection and diagnosis– abnormalities and unforeseen events are simulated. The control room operator is required to understand the situation, determine a recovery plan, replan upcoming activities and communicate with all relevant teams and document the situation. Detection, diagnosis and communications will typically involve discussion with other control centres, engineering support, maintenance and relevant scientists.

These are used for initial assessments to certify control room operators' competence as well as ongoing assessment to maintain competence required for certification. The simulations also act as powerful refresher training to help maintain knowledge development.

Case study 12: On-the-job assessments

A UK nuclear power plant developed on-the-job initial and ongoing assessments of CROs' knowledge and skill. The assessments were developed, written in parallel with procedural documentation, so that each procedure has dedicated on-the job training along with assessments that need to be undertaken, initially as part of the training and then periodically to ensure competence. This ensures the assessments (and training) are focused on the necessary task demands.

The assessment is split into two parts:

Part one – Assessment of the operator's knowledge and understanding

A series of questions aim to determine if the operators have achieved the required level of underpinning knowledge and understanding of the process i.e. why tasks are conducted, why tasks are conducted in a specific sequence, why certain steps are considered critical and the unsafe conditions that the critical steps are protecting against. Example questions include: 'What are the [action] checks protecting against?'; 'Why should the label be removed or made illegible at the end of [an action]?'; 'Why is there an independent check required when entering data onto the computer system?'.

Part two – Assessment of the operator's skills

A set of skill based assessment criteria is used by assessors to determine, through observation, if operators are competent to carry out a process. Example skill based assessment criteria include: 'The trainee should demonstrate use of the motorised tunnel as part of a shipment move, involving:
- conducting motorised tunnel and trolley checks prior to use;
- entering details of the shipment move onto the computer system;
- waits and checks. . .'

This method of assessment helps the organisation assure that CROs have acquired and can demonstrate the required knowledge and skill to perform their jobs safely and efficiently.

Case study 13: Written and picture based assessments

A multinational gas company uses written tests and picture based scenarios to test technical and non-technical skills and knowledge during abnormal conditions.

Written multiple choice tests are used to assess technical and non-technical knowledge relating to abnormal conditions. This includes relevant engineering, safe systems of work and operating procedures for these conditions. A pass mark of 90 % is required. For those who do not pass, targeted coaching is provided by an assessor, with a follow-up exam, using different questions administered within a set time period.

Picture based scenarios are then used to help assess non-technical skills, in terms of ability to understand risks, diagnose the problem, select the correct solutions and communicate them clearly. The desktop scenarios are run in small groups, with each person tasked with managing the response until the scenario has ended. The scenarios are all based on abnormal conditions that have occurred within the organisation.

Competencies are assessed using technical skill and non-technical skill anchors. The assessor will also ask the individual to talk through their decisions and actions as a further test of technical and non-technical knowledge.

This assessment is triangulated with any report of on-the-job performance data relating to the individual's management of abnormal conditions. Based on this information, judgements on competence are made and areas for development communicated. Where the individuals are judged as 'not competent' on any area, targeted coaching and mentoring is put in place, with reassessment scheduled.

7   RETAIN AND SUPPORT CROs

Having selected, trained and assessed CROs, retention of established and advanced CROs and realising the benefits from investment of time and effort into producing competent CROs becomes the next challenge.

This section focuses on enhancing CRO retention through strengthening the organisational arrangements that support CROs. It covers the following topics:
- creating CRO retention plans;
- enhancing retention through:
  - leadership;
  - management and supervision of CROs;
  - improving the design of control rooms and associated operating procedures, and
  - managing change.

7.1   CREATE A CRO RETENTION PLAN

An explicit retention plan can be developed, detailing the types of activities and processes to help retain CROs (Deery, 2008). Table 12 provides example retention activities that can be included within a retention plan.

Table 12: Example retention activities

Example activities	Description
Creating a career path	Provide a clear career path for CROs. CROs may become frustrated if they cannot see a clear career path. This requires the development of clear goals, linked to career aspirations and utilisation of different techniques such as shadowing and job rotation.
Developing new skills	Provide established and advanced CROs with opportunities to develop new skills, not just refreshing and reassessing current skills.
Fostering ownership	Provide CROs with opportunities for ownership. This could be ownership over their own learning, for example, through a distance learning course or access to a simulator to practise tasks. It could be ownership over certain responsibilities and activities.
Building connections	Make it clear to CROs how their role helps achieve business/ operational unit objectives. This can be achieved through toolbox talks or informal discussions. This may help CROs feel connected to the organisation's goals.
Providing benefits	Where possible offer CROs a range of competitive benefits. This should not only include financial benefits but might also include other benefits such as healthcare, flexi-time and help where possible to achieve work-life balance.

Table 12: Example retention activities (continued)

Example activities	Description
Providing small perks	Where possible, CROs should be provided with small perks. Small perks, such as paying for breakfast, were implemented in the construction of the Olympic Park in the UK, with great success[2].
Setting expectations	Make it clear what will be expected of CROs if they are selected for the role and the type of opportunities that will be provided to them, as well as their level of autonomy in their role. If expectations are not managed correctly, CROs may feel demotivated or lose trust in the organisation.

7.2 RETAINING CROs

Figure 4 illustrates a set of organisational arrangements that may enhance retention, by supporting CROs.

Figure 4: Factors to help CRO retention

---

2   http://www.hse.gov.uk/aboutus/london-2012-games/research-reports.htm

7.2.1 Leadership

Relevant leaders can help CROs feel valued by demonstrating commitment to CRO competence management (IAEA-TECDOC-1479). Ways to achieve this include:
- Appoint a member of the senior management team with overall responsibility for the competence management of CROs.
- Relevant senior managers should agree a set of key performance indicators (KPIs) for CRO competence management.
- Relevant leaders should create an environment where CRO competence management is seen as a continual process.
- Relevant leaders should demonstrate commitment to ongoing competence development of CROs, for example, attending CRO training and carrying out regular safety conversations/walk-throughs of control rooms to explore opportunities for enhancing CRO competence management.
- Carry out regular interviews to understand why CROs stay within the organisation. This can help you identify new ways of retaining CROs.

7.2.2 Supervision and management

Supervisors and managers can create a positive working environment for CROs, which can increase CRO commitment. Supervisors and managers can:
- Help identify training needs and provide opportunities for ongoing competence development.
- Ensure CROs clearly understand their role and the impact their action and decisions can have on the control of major accident hazards.
- Be involved and ideally, where applicable, carry out training and assessments of CRO competence, particularly on-the-job training and assessment.
- Effectively manage CRO break times, ensuring competent cover is provided for breaks.
- Encourage peer-to-peer learning, assessment and mentoring and provide opportunities for this to happen, for example, peer mentoring or setting self-directed peer learning assignments.
- Mentor, coach and buddy CROs.
- Actively involve CROs, where possible, in decisions such as procurement of equipment, revision of procedures, shift patterns, health and safety improvements etc.
- Carry out pre- and post- training discussions, with focus on how the CRO can demonstrate their learning in the control room, and identifying ongoing development opportunities.
- Identify and tackle, or escalate to senior managers, factors that can affect the performance of CROs. Such factors might include staffing levels, workload, team working, job design and personal issues.

(IAEA-TECDOC-1479; Leach et al, 2011)

Supervisors and managers should also be provided with relevant training and assessments to ensure they develop the non-technical knowledge and skills required to effectively support CROs.

7.2.3   Procedures

Procedures support CROs by providing the information they require to carry out their duties safely, efficiently and reliably across routine, infrequent, abnormal and emergency responses (Hsieh et al, 2012; Selfe et al, 2012). To achieve this, procedures should:
–   Be clear and unambiguous with critical tasks clearly identified.
–   Be up-to date and achievable, i.e. CROs can apply them within the control room to complete tasks within a certain time limit.
–   Provide content, level of detail and structure that is based on the task type, criticality, frequency and complexity of the task and knowledge and skills required. For example, routine and infrequent tasks may be described in detail within procedures, with supporting diagrams and schematics. Emergency response tasks that rely heavily on non-technical skills and dynamic decision making may be better described in usable job aids, supported by detailed ongoing practical based training and development.
–   Be developed by people with the necessary knowledge, skills and experience, i.e. those with the detailed understanding of CRO tasks and responsibilities as well as knowledge of what makes effective and usable procedures.
–   Be developed and reviewed with the involvement of CROs.
–   Support the decision making process of CROs and where applicable describe cognitive activities, such as fault diagnosis in abnormal conditions, and factors to consider when prioritising information and making decisions.
–   Be supported by relevant training describing why tasks are completed in specific ways and the hazards and risks being controlled by the procedure.

It should be noted that shortfalls in the design of control room systems and interfaces should not be compensated for through procedures.

7.2.4   Control room design

Effective control room design can help reduce CRO stress. This is because well-designed control rooms help CROs form a clear and holistic mental picture of plant and process (Larson, 2012), allowing them to more effectively undertake critical tasks and manage workload.

Design decisions should be informed by human factors assessments, with explicit involvement of control room operators. Human factors assessments should be completed throughout the design process, particularly early on. Typical human factors activities that could be completed include:
–   Understanding the specific operator activities, characteristics and requirements relevant to the design. For example, determining how the operator will interact with the system and will support their decision making.
–   Identifying relevant safety issues. For example, identifying the potential risk, hazards and errors that are associated with the operator's activities.
–   Analysing and prioritising relevant safety issues. For example, identifying the issues that are most important in relation to operator decision making and determining which issues can be addressed through the design.
–   Testing and evaluating design solutions, with control room operators. For example, determining the extent to which the solution reduces the known safety issue or introduces a new risk or hazard.

Table 13 provides example design requirements to support control room operators (Kempf and Glathe, 2012; The Engineering Equipment and Materials Users' Association, *Alarm systems: A guide to design, management and procurement*).

Table 13: Example design requirements

Example control room design requirements
Overview displays with essential operating parameters to be monitored, display of tolerances, safe operating envelopes and hierarchy of importance used to help organise displays.
Standardisation and prioritised alarms, using distinct alarms, colours and sounds.
Visualised process information provided so that the operator can understand the event taking place and undertake appropriate action.
Clear approach to acknowledgement of alarms. For example, low to medium priority alarms can revert to quiet mode without corrective actions, but should reactivate after a period of time if they have not been addressed.
Avoidance of cognitive overload.
As far as possible, consistent design of control panels, control devices and display screens. For example, conforming to the same rules in terms of colour coding, location of buttons etc.
Navigation between different screens and displayed information is intuitive, clearly labelled and compatible with the CROs' understanding and expectation of the system and how it should behave. For example, the order of display screens is compatible with the mental model of how an operator views and perceives information.
Jump function from alarm page to the measuring point in the process picture along with functionality to access and drill-down on schematics and diagrams.
Displays for 'pattern support' and trends to help decide on operating strategy.
Critical feedback information displayed, so operator can determine if actions are successful.
Screen layouts are divided into zones, such as header bar, menu bar and content area. Each area conforms to the same rules to make it easier for the control room operator to locate information.
Uniform and device-neutral presentation of the operator screen forms, and use of the same input and output devices as for process control to support correct entering of information.
Presentation of all relevant process values to support log keeping.
Visualisation of quality KPIs in overview displays of the process control to support the quality management of process control.
Controls provide feedback through a visual or auditory response (e.g. an audible click) following action by the control room operator. Feedback should be immediate (within 100 milliseconds).
Controls are distinct in their design, meaningfully labelled and an adequate distance apart.
Controls provide the opportunity for error recovery, for example, use pop-up menus with a warning that requires confirmation before the control room operator can fully implement an action, where relevant.

7.2.5 Change management

Change can affect how CROs perform and their level of commitment to an organisation. Where applicable, any change should be assessed, as far as reasonably practicable, to determine if it can affect CRO tasks, their competence requirements and/or the processes in place to manage CRO competence. Example changes might include:

– Downsizing and delaying, affecting staffing levels, management and supervision arrangements.
– Changes to production processes, for example type of products being developed, method of production, volume of products, batch processes etc.
– Changes to control room design, for example displays, equipment, controls.
– Recommendations from an incident and/or accident investigation either within the organisation or relevant industry relating to the CRO tasks and their competence requirements.
– Introduction of new regulation and/or NOSs, or revision to existing regulation and standards relating to the management of CRO competence.
– Changes to CRO job profiles or the risk profile of the organisation.
– Changes to shift patterns.

If it is identified that a change may potentially have this effect, a review of the CRO competence management system should take place (see section 8). The extent to which CRO knowledge and expertise may be lost as part of the change should also be assessed. Such knowledge can be captured and transferred, through methods such as peer coaching, peer-led toolbox talks and detailed exit interviews.

7.3 CASE STUDIES

Case study 14: Leadership

To demonstrate commitment to CRO competence management, the senior management team of a gas distribution company attended the non-technical skills training being delivered to all staff, including CROs.

At the end of every non-technical skills training session held, several members of the senior management team would hold a question and answer session with the trainees, focusing on identifying the organisational systems that hindered job performance, with the aim of enhancing these systems, to ensure staff could perform to the best of their ability. The question and answer sessions were also used to communicate the changes the senior management team had already put in place to support CROs.

Case study 15: Supervisor development

A multinational energy company identified a set of non-technical knowledge and skills that supervisors and managers required to support non-technical skills training. These included:
- knowledge of non-technical skills required for critical roles and how these should be documented;
- understanding/appreciation of human factors and the factors that can affect performance;
- self-awareness and objective observation;
- being a good listener and clear communicator;
- assertiveness and confidence in challenging unsafe behaviour or poor performance;
- coaching skills and ability to motivate, and
- positive approach to learning, especially learning from mistakes.

Before non-technical skills training was provided to front-line staff, the company developed and delivered a specific course for supervisors and managers, focused on developing the knowledge and skills described here. The course covered the importance of the supervisors and managers in developing competence and the impact they can have on effective learning and development, and involved practical sessions for developing skills and applying knowledge.

Case study 16: Change management

A refinery was undertaking a range of changes including combining certain production processes and reducing staffing levels.

As part of the process, a set of change workshops were undertaken with process safety engineers to understand the effect these changes could have on control room operations and CROs.

Two main assessments took place:
1. Staffing level assessments to determine the safe level of staffing required for combined production processes, and the effect on workload, supervision and available time for competence development and assessment.
2. CRO competence management review to determine the effect the change would have on CRO tasks, their competence requirements and arrangements for competence management, and to identify relevant changes that needed to take place to ensure CRO competence management arrangements remained up to date, reliable, valid and could still be applied with reduced staff numbers.

8 MONITOR AND REVIEW CRO COMPETENCE MANAGEMENT ARRANGEMENTS

This section focuses on how to monitor and review CRO competence management arrangements, covering:
- carrying out a review;
- ensuring the review is underpinned by accurate and reliable criteria, and
- using multiple sources of information.

8.1 CARRY OUT A REVIEW

To help achieve an accurate review that identifies valid areas of improvement, the organisation should:
- Review against clearly defined criteria, mapped to major accident hazards, covering good practice in the competence management of CROs.
- Use risk based indicators to determine the frequency, with greater frequency targeted towards areas of concern.
- Use and review lessons learnt from accidents, incidents, injuries, near misses, process upset conditions etc, within and outside the CRO's organisation.
- Train reviewers so they can use multiple methods and evidence for review.
- Involve CROs, their trainers, assessors, supervisors and relevant managers.
- Assess improvements to understand effectiveness.
- Review the review process, including criteria, frequency and methods used etc, to ensure that it is valid, accurate and can identify areas of improvement.

Annex C provides a checklist self-assessment to help determine the effectiveness of the organisation's arrangements for managing CRO competence.

8.2 EXAMPLE REVIEW CRITERIA

Good practice (HSE, *Competence assessment for the hazardous industries;* HSE, *Inspectors toolkit: Human factors in the management of major accident hazards*) describes three critical elements for reviewing competence arrangements:
- Competence standards – extent to which CRO competence management arrangements are underpinned by an accurate and valid description of CRO competence requirements.
- Training – extent to which CRO competence management arrangements provide training that develops the right knowledge and technical and non-technical skills, so they perform to the standard required.
- Assessment – extent to which CRO competence management arrangements provide accurate and valid assessments.

8.2.1 Competence standards

The organisation should consider the extent to which CRO competence standards:
- Prioritise critical CRO tasks.
- Describe the knowledge, technical and non-technical skills required to complete critical CRO tasks, and provide measurable statements of performance for CRO critical tasks, for each CRO development stage.

Example sources of information that can be used to help review competence standards include:

- CRO critical task analysis.
- Risk assessments (such as a hazard and operability studies (HAZOP), 'what if' analysis) carried out as part of safety case relating to control room operations and CRO critical tasks.
- CRO job analysis and training needs analysis.
- Safety case and safety management system reviews, including identifying emergency scenarios (and process upsets/abnormal operating states) and critical tasks for which CROs' competence should be assessed.
- CRO critical procedures, task and job descriptions.
- Relevant error analysis carried out on CRO safety criticality of tasks or operations, such as those generated through quantitative risk analysis.
- CRO task inventories and competence standards.
- Current plant risk registers relating to control room operations and CRO critical tasks.
- CRO measurable statements of performance.
- Relevant near misses, incidents and accidents and process upsets/abnormalities that relate to control room operations and CRO tasks, competencies, performance expectations and training needs.
- NOSs, NVQs or any other national standards that have been used to help develop CRO competence standards and help to describe CRO tasks, competencies, performance expectations and training needs.
- Interviews with CROs, supervisors and relevant managers and subject matter experts within the organisation, for example safety team, risk management, human resource, etc.
- Risk assessments that have been carried out as part of change management, relating to control room operations, CRO task competencies, performance expectations and training needs.
- Industry incidents and accidents that have occurred relating to control room operations, CRO task competencies, performance expectations and training needs.

8.2.2 Training

The organisation should consider the extent to which training is:

- Matched to CRO task criticality, complexity, frequency of task performance and CRO stages of development.
- Accurate, up to date and reflects the roles and responsibilities of CROs.
- Using a variety of appropriate training methods matched to the task type and competence requirements of CROs.
- Structured around principles of adult learning.
- Developed and delivered by suitably trained and qualified trainers.
- Associated with observed improvements in CRO performance and relevant measures of organisational performance, i.e. performance indicators that can be influenced by the competence of CROs, such as time taken to restore production after a process upset.

Example sources of information that can be used to help review training include:

- CRO critical task analysis, job analysis, training needs analysis and CRO critical procedures to help validate frequency, type and content of training.
- Post-training interviews and questionnaires administered to CROs, supervisors and trainers to understand satisfaction with CRO training, impact on performance and identification of strengths and areas for improvement.

- All CRO training materials including CRO talent management arrangements; methods and types of training; CRO learning objectives.
- All CRO competence assessment records and judgement of competence to understand effectiveness of training and potential training needs. CRO competence assessments should be compared before and after relevant training and refresher training to understand impact on CRO competence.
- On-the-job CRO performance and behaviours, including near misses, incidents and accidents relating to CRO competence, number of process upset conditions relating to CRO performance, speed of detection, diagnosis and recovery; extent to which CRO operational performance targets are met, CRO safety audit performance, CRO levels of procedural compliance.
- Good practice in training and development including research on principles of adult learning taken from a range of industries. This can include the introduction of new standards and regulations and/or revisions in standards and regulations.
- Number of CROs deemed 'not competent' and trends across a number of years.
- Existing trainer competencies, methods for selection, assessment and ongoing competence management as well as associated job analysis, measurable standards and training needs developed for trainers. This should be compared against relevant best practice, standards and training approaches for trainers, taken from different industries.
- Incidents and accidents across different industries that have occurred relating to CRO training and competence, and areas for improvement.
- Relevant near misses, incident, accidents and process upsets/abnormalities that have happened in the organisation related to control room operations and tasks.

8.2.3 Assessment

The organisation should consider the extent to which CRO assessments:
- cover all procedures and processes that are relevant to critical tasks;
- address all required technical and non-technical skill and knowledge for critical task completion;
- use a range of methods that are appropriate to the critical task and competence requirements of CROs;
- are guided by measurable statements of performance, and
- are delivered by competent assessors.

This element is also focused on assessing the system in place to manage CROs judged to be 'not competent' and how training and supervision is provided to ensure CROs reach the desired level of competence without compromising plant safety.

Example sources of information that can be used to help review assessments include:
- CRO training, safety-critical task analysis, job analysis and training needs analysis as well as CRO critical procedures to validate content of assessments.
- CROs', supervisors' and assessors' satisfaction with reliability, validity and fairness of CRO assessments. This can be gathered through interviews and/or post-assessment questionnaires.
- CRO assessment criteria and measurable statements of performance compared to the previous point to help determine accuracy.
- On-the-job performance data, for example, near misses, incidents and accidents relating to CRO competence, process upset conditions relating to CRO performance; safety audit and other performance review systems to identify CRO competence problems; CRO operational performance targets, CRO safety audit performance, CRO levels of procedural compliance.

- All CRO assessments, assessment plans and CRO assessment records, including action plans and reassessments. This should include comparisons of assessments across different assessors to understand reliability of assessment and of assessors' judgements.
- Time taken to bring CROs deemed 'not competent' to required levels of competence and trends across a number of years.
- Relevant NOSs and regulations used to inform assessments and frequency of reassessment. This will help assess validity and accuracy of assessments.
- Existing assessor competencies, methods for selection, assessment and ongoing competence management as well as associated job analysis, measurable standards and training needs developed for assessors. This should be compared against relevant best practice, standards and training approaches, for assessors taken from different industries.
- Industry incidents and accidents that have highlighted weaknesses in CRO competence assessments and areas for improvement.
- Relevant near misses, incidents, accidents and process upsets/abnormalities that have happened in the organisation related to control room operations and CRO tasks. These can highlight weaknesses in CRO competence assessments and areas for improvement.
- Best practice in competence assessment taken from a range of industries. This can include the introduction of new standards and regulations and/or revisions in standards and regulations.

8.3   CASE STUDIES

Case study 17: Standardised review

A multinational gas company uses a standardised approach to reviewing the competence management arrangements of operators including CROs. The review process focuses on:
- Risks – how CRO critical tasks, relevant competencies and measurable standards are identified and developed and how these clearly link to major accident hazards and occupational health and safety risks.
- Procedures – how CRO critical tasks and competencies are described in CRO procedures, how these procedures are developed and how procedures are used to help control major accident hazards.
- Training – how CRO training is identified, developed and delivered and the effectiveness of this training in terms of CRO knowledge development, job performance and organisational improvements.
- Review – how accurate the overall review process is in terms of competence of reviewers, effectiveness of communications of findings and extent to which review criteria are linked to major accident hazards and occupational health and safety risk.
- Change – how the competence management arrangements are reviewed when change takes place, extent to which these arrangements are updated and the effectiveness of these updates to ensure the CRO competence management arrangements help to manage risks associated with change.

The review process includes direct labour and relevant sub-contractors, and takes place every three years or when a major change takes place. This may include a change to equipment, process or working practice.

ANNEX A
REFERENCES AND FURTHER RESOURCES

A.1   REFERENCES

Health and Safety Executive (HSE) (http://www.hse.gov.uk)

COMAH Competent Authority, Inspection of competence management systems at COMAH establishments. Operational delivery guide

CRR 348/2001 *Assessing the safety of staffing arrangements for process operations in the chemical and allied industries*

Competence assessment for the hazardous industries. Research Report 086
Inspectors toolkit. Human factors in the management of major accident hazards

Rail Safety and Standards Board (http://www.rssb.co.uk)

Good practice guide on competence development. Document No RS/100 issue 1

Risk based training needs analysis. Guide to the process and templates

Operations and management: Review of GB driver training and development of leading practice models for the industry. Guide to the process and template

Energy Institute (EI) (http://www.energyinst.org)

Guidance on human factors safety critical task analysis

Guidance on meeting expectations of EI Process safety management framework Element 3: Employee selection, placement and competency, and health assurance

International Atomic Energy Agency (http://www.iaea.org)

IAEA-TECDOC-1411, *Use of control room simulators for training of nuclear power plant personnel*

IAEA-TECDOC-1502, *Authorization of nuclear power plant control room personnel: Methods and practices with emphasis on the use of simulators*

IAEA-TECDOC-1479, *Human performance improvement in organisations: Potential application for the nuclear industry*

Other authors

Berger, L. and Berger, R. (2011) *The talent management handbook: Creating a sustainable competitive advantage by selecting, developing, and promoting the best people.* McGraw-Hill Professional

Buckley, R and Caple, C. (2004) *The theory and practice of training.* Kogan Page: London
Cogent/UKPIA, *Guidelines for competency management systems for downstream and petroleum sites*

Cook, M. (2004) *Personnel selection. Adding value through people.* John Wiley and Sons Ltd. USA

Deery, M. (2008) *Talent management, work-life balance and retention strategies.* Emerald 20

Doyle, C (2003) *Work and organisational psychology. An introduction with attitude.* Psychology Press. Hove

Hsieh, M., Hwang, S., Liu, K., Liang, S., and Chuang, C. (2012) *A decision support system for identifying abnormal operating procedures in a nuclear power plant*. Nuclear Engineering and Design. Vol 249. pp 413–418

Jarvis, P., Holford, J. and Griffin, C. (2003) *The theory and practice of learning*. 2nd ed. London; Sterling, Va.: Kogan Page

Kempf, S., and Glathe, L. (2012) *Modern plant control centers and operator control concepts* A white paper issued by Siemens. © Siemens AG 2012

Kim, S. and Byun, S. (2011) *Effects of crew resource management training on the team performance of operators in an advanced nuclear power plant*, Journal of Nuclear Science and Technology, Vol 48. Issue 9. Pp 1256–1264

Kluge, A. and Burkolter, D. (2010) *Comparative study of three training methods for enhancing process control performance: Emphasis shift training, situation awareness training, and drill and practice*. Computers in Human Behavior. Vol 26. Issue 5. pp 976–986

Kluge, A., and Burkolter, D. (2008) *Training principles for process control tasks and innovative approaches to training*, found at http://www.psychologie.uzh.ch/fachrichtungen/angpsy/biaesch/gesuche/Kluge_Burkolter.pdf

Krause, K.D, Bochner, S. and Duchesnes, S. (2002) *Educational psychology for learning and teaching*. South Melbourne: Thomson Learning

Larson, K. (2012) *Operator effectiveness: The next frontier of process automation*, ABB and Control White Paper

Leach, P., Berman, J. and Goodall, D. (2011) *Achieving compliance through people: Training supervisors to tackle procedural non-compliance*. Paper presented at Hazards XXII: Process safety and environmental protection, Liverpool: IChemE

Marcella, R., Pirie, T., and Doig, D. (2011) *Tick safety not boxes: Competency and compliance in the oil and gas industry*. Aberdeen Business School. Research commissioned by OPITO

Selfe, R., Watson, S., Sheridan A. and Berman J. (2012) *Where do procedures sit within a competence management system?* Paper presented at Hazards XXIII, Southport: IChemE

The Engineering Equipment and Materials Users' Association, *Alarm systems: A guide to design, management and procurement*. Publication No 191. Edition 2

Wright, M., Berman, J. and Turner, D. (2003) *Competence assessment and major accident prevention*. Institute of Chemical Engineers, Symposium Series No.149

A.2 FURTHER RESOURCES

In addition to the references cited, the following materials may also be useful to the reader:

A.2.1 Determine CRO competence requirements

Cogent Final Approved ACG 12. *Assessment strategy for the chemical, pharmaceutical, nuclear, oil and gas, petroleum and polymer industries*

European Chemical Employee Group. *European framework agreement on competence profiles for process operators and first line supervisors in the chemical industry*

Finnish Radiation and Nuclear Safety Authority (STUK). *Qualification of control room operators for nuclear power plants*

National Occupational Standard: COGDO30. *Control room operations in downstream operations*

National Occupational Standard: COGPIO3.1. *Control room operations in processing industries operations*

OPITO Approved Standard Code 9004. *Control room operator emergency response standard*

OPITO approved standard. *Offshore oil and gas Industry transformation scheme process program training standard*

OPITO International issue 1. *Guidance for effective management of competence and training in emergency response in the oil and gas industry*

OPITO National Occupational Standards for FPSO/FSUs. *Marine technician operations critical and emergency situations*

OPITO National Occupational Standards for Processing Operations Hydrocarbon. *Control room operator involved with oil and gas production*

Scottish Qualifications Authority. *Assessor's guidelines for the SVQ in processing operations: Hydrocarbons at level 1,*

Scottish Qualifications Authority. *Assessor's guidelines for the SVQ in processing operations: Hydrocarbons at level 2*

Scottish Qualifications Authority. *Assessor's guidelines for the SVQ in processing operations: Hydrocarbons at level 3*

Scottish Qualifications Authority. *Assessor's guidelines for the SVQ in processing operations: Processing Operations: Hydrocarbons (Control Room) at level 3*

A.2.2   Train CROs

Blass, E. (2009) *Talent management: Cases and commentary*, Palgrave Macmillan

Calo, T. (2008) *Talent management in the era of the aging workforce. The critical role of knowledge transfer*. Public personnel management. Vol 37. No. 4. Pp 403–416

Centre of Excellence for Energy Technology. *Power generation skill standard. Plant operators and plant mechanics*

HSE, *Development of a multiskilling life cycle mode*. Research Report 328

Lewis, R. and Heckman, R. (2006) *Talent management: A critical review*. Human resource management review, 16, pp 139–145

Manca, D., Nazir, S., and Colombo, S. (2012) *Performance indicators for training assessment of control-room operators*. Chemical Engineering Transactions. Vol 26. The Italian Association of Chemical Engineering

Shukla, R. (2009) *Talent management: Process of developing and integrating skilled workers*. Global. India Publications Pvt Ltd.

A.2.3   Assess CROs

Cogent/UKPIA, *Guidelines for competency management systems for downstream and petroleum sites*

Danielsen, B. and Stene, T. (2013) *Control room operations and certification for space operations*. In *Safety, reliability and risk analysis. Beyond the Horizon*. Eds: Steenbergen, R, Van Gelder, P, Miraglia, S. and Vrouwenvelder, A. (2013) CRC Press

European Process Safety Centre. *Process safety competence. How to set up a process safety competence management system*. Report Number 35

Office for Nuclear Regulation (ONR) of the Health and Safety Executive. *Technical assessment guide: Assessment of licensee's arrangements for training and assuring personnel competence*. T/AST/027- Issue 3

A.2.4 Retain and support CROs

Flin, R. (2005) *Safe in their hands? Licensing and competence assurance for safety-critical roles in high risk industries*. University of Aberdeen. Report for the Department of Health

Flin, R. (2013) *The power of behaviour: Non-technical skills*. Jan de Kroes Lecture. Industrial Psychology Research Centre, University of Aberdeen, Scotland

HSE, *Factoring the human into safety: Translating research into practice. Crew resource management*. Research Report No 061

Parkes, K. (2000) *Sleep patterns, shiftwork, and individual differences: A Comparison of onshore and offshore control-room operators*. Journal of Human Performance in Extreme Environments. Vol 6. Iss 1. Article 8

Roe, E., and Schulman P. (2011). *A high reliability management perspective on the Deepwater Horizon spill, including research implications*. Deepwater Horizon Study Group 3 Working Paper

RSSB. *Good practice guide: Competence retention. T717. A model for competence retention in rail industry (skill fade)*

A.2.5 Monitor and review CRO competence arrangements

Eurocontrol. *Guidelines for competence assessment. European air traffic management programme*. Edition 2

Flin, R. (2005) *Safe in their hands? Licensing and competence assurance for safety-critical roles in high risk industries*. University of Aberdeen. Report for the Department of Health

HSE. *Assessing the safety of staffing arrangements for process operations in the chemical and allied industries*. Research Report No 348

RSSB. *Good practice guide: Competence retention. T717. A model for competence retention in rail industry (skill fade)*

ANNEX B
GLOSSARY OF ABREVIATIONS AND ACRONYMS

CIT	critical incident technique
COMAH	Control of Major Accident Hazards
CRM	crew resource management
CRO	control room operator
CTTLS	certificate in teaching in the lifelong learning sector
EDS	electrostatic discharge system
EI	Energy Institute
HAZOP	hazard and operability study
HOFCOM	Energy Institute Human and Organisational Factors Committee
HSE	Health and Safety Executive
HSEQ	health, safety, environment and quality
IAEA	International Atomic Energy Agency
IOSH	Institution of Occupational Safety and Health
KPI	key performance indicator
NOS	National Occupational Standard
NVQ	National Vocational Qualification
ONR	Office for Nuclear Regulation
OPITO	Offshore Petroleum Industry Training Organization
PTLLS	preparing to teach in the lifelong learning sector
RSSB	Rail Safety Standards Board
SCADA	supervisory control and data acquisition
STUK	Finnish Radiation and Nuclear Safety Authority
UKPIA	UK Petroleum Industry Association

ANNEX C
SELF-ASSESSMENT CHECKLIST

This annex contains self-assessments for:
a)   Understanding key challenges faced ensuring the competence of CROs. This may be of particular interest for:
- Relevant members of training, human resources, learning and development, talent management functions, for example, those responsible for CRO training and assessment.
- Internal auditors responsible for auditing CRO competence and/or competence management arrangements.
b)   Those reviewing CRO competence management arrangements. This may be of particular interest for:
- Internal auditors responsible for auditing CRO competence and/or competence management arrangements.
- Relevant members of HSEQ who influence and/or monitor CRO operations.

C.1   UNDERSTANDING YOUR CHALLENGES

This self-assessment aims to help you think about the challenges faced when ensuring CRO competence. It can be used to identify those elements that are of most interest/concern, and determine which sections of the guide are most relevant. The questions are intended to be answered using a 'traffic light' score. Yellow and red indicate areas for consideration. Green indicates areas that should be continued and fully supported.

Table C.1: Challenge 1 – Using CRO standards and regulations to determine CRO competence requirements

Questions	Yes	To some extent	No	Relevant section(s) of EI *Guidance on ensuring control room operator (CRO) competence*
1. Are you able to effectively incorporate your specific CRO competence requirements with those described in CRO standards and regulations?	☐	☐	☐	If mainly yellow and red go to: **4: Determine CRO competence requirements**
2. Are you confident that you utilise national CRO standards and regulations in the best possible way to support the training and development of CROs?	☐	☐	☐	
3. Can you accurately determine which regulations and standards should be used for your CROs?	☐	☐	☐	
4. Are you able to apply CRO standards and regulations in a practical way to enhance CRO competence?	☐	☐	☐	

Table C.2: Challenge 2 – Assessing potential to become beginner CRO

Questions	Yes	To some extent	No	Relevant section(s) of EI *Guidance on ensuring control room operator (CRO) competence*
1. Are you confident that your pool of candidates with the potential to perform the role of a CRO is as strong as it can/should be?	☐	☐	☐	If mainly yellow and red go to: **6: Assess CROs**
2. Do you accurately define the underpinning skills and attitudes to assess the potential of people to become beginner CROs?	☐	☐	☐	
3. Do you assess the potential of people to become beginner CROs and if so, has it proved to be accurate?	☐	☐	☐	

Table C.3: Challenge 3 – Training, assessment and assurance of beginner to advanced CROs

Questions	Yes	To some extent	No	Relevant section(s) of EI *Guidance on ensuring control room operator (CRO) competence*
1. Are you confident that you have identified and validated the right knowledge, technical and non-technical skills for CROs, across normal, infrequent, abnormal and emergency response situations?	☐	☐	☐	If mainly yellow and red go to: **4: Determine CRO competence requirements** **5: Train CROs** **6: Assess CROs**
2. Are you confident that you have identified and validated the right knowledge, technical and non-technical skills for CROs, across each stage from beginner to advanced?	☐	☐	☐	
3. Do you consider potential major accident hazards, across normal, infrequent, abnormal and emergency response situations when identifying and validating CRO competencies?	☐	☐	☐	
4. Do you assess competence, to inform CRO selection decisions?	☐	☐	☐	

Table C.3: Challenge 3 – Training, assessment and assurance of beginner to advanced CROs (continued)

Questions	Yes	To some extent	No	Relevant section(s) of EI *Guidance on ensuring control room operator (CRO) competence*
5. Are you confident that CRO training and assessments are accurately matched to the right competencies, across normal, infrequent, abnormal and emergency response situations?	☐	☐	☐	
6. Are you confident that CRO training and assessments are accurately matched to the right competencies, across each stage from beginner to advanced?	☐	☐	☐	
7. Do you use process simulators, simulation and/or other realistic training environments across normal, infrequent, abnormal and emergency response situations to develop and assess CRO competence?	☐	☐	☐	
8. A) Do you carry out ongoing assessments of CRO competence once they have become established and/or advanced?	☐	☐	☐	
8. B) If so, do you believe they are as effective as they can be?	☐	☐	☐	
9. A) Have you identified the competence requirements of CRO trainers and assessors?	☐	☐	☐	
9. B) If so, do you provide them with ongoing training and assessment they require?	☐	☐	☐	

Table C.4: Challenge 4 – Retaining and supporting CROs

Questions	Yes	To some extent	No	Relevant section(s) of EI *Guidance on ensuring control room operator (CRO) competence*
1. Do you regularly audit the competence management arrangements of CROs?	☐	☐	☐	If mainly yellow and red go to: **7: Retain and support CROs** **8: Monitor and review CRO competence management arrangements**
2. Are you confident that the audit process will help you to determine the extent to which CRO training and assessment are fit-for-purpose?	☐	☐	☐	
3. Do you retain the majority of your CROs?	☐	☐	☐	
4. Do relevant leaders and/ or supervisors demonstrate commitment and support to the competence management of CROs?	☐	☐	☐	
5. Do you assess the impact plant/ equipment/staffing changes have on the training and assessment provided to CROs?	☐	☐	☐	
6. Do the following support your CROs to carry out their tasks safely, efficiently and reliably:				
Supervisors	☐	☐	☐	
Procedures	☐	☐	☐	
Staffing levels	☐	☐	☐	
Workload	☐	☐	☐	
Automation	☐	☐	☐	
Alarms and alerts	☐	☐	☐	

C.2 REVIEWING CRO COMPETENCE MANAGEMENT ARRANGEMENTS

This self-assessment allows you to assess the organisation against example criteria for reviewing CRO competence management arrangements. The questions use a 'traffic light' score system. Yellow and red indicate areas for consideration for improvement. Green indicates areas that should be continued and fully supported.

Table C.5: – Safety-critical task analysis and competence requirements

Example criteria statement	Yes	To some extent	No
1. All CRO safety-critical tasks that affect or initiate major accident hazards for routine, infrequent, abnormal and emergency response operations have been identified and described.	☐	☐	☐
2. The safety case has been reviewed to identify emergency scenarios (and process upsets/ abnormal operating states) and CRO safety-critical tasks.	☐	☐	☐
3. CRO competence requirements, measurable standards and training needs have been established for routine, infrequent, abnormal and emergency response operations and per CRO development stage as required.	☐	☐	☐
4. The necessary underpinning knowledge and skills for equipment, processes, hazards and consequences are described for all CRO safety-critical tasks for routine, infrequent, abnormal and emergency response operations.	☐	☐	☐
5. CRO task inventories have been prepared for all tasks that have the potential to contribute to a major accident.	☐	☐	☐
6. Safety-critical task analysis, job analysis and task inventories have been cross-referenced to risk assessments (such as a HAZOP, What if? analysis or safety reviews) for validation.	☐	☐	☐
7. CRO NOSs, NVQs and any other national standards have been developed to match site-specific risks and CRO competence requirements.	☐	☐	☐
8. Changes that affect CRO safety-critical tasks, competencies, measurable standards and training needs are identified, with necessary amendments to CRO competence management arrangements actioned.	☐	☐	☐

Table C.6: – Training

Example criteria statement	Yes	To some extent	No
1. Training for beginner to advanced CROs is accurate, up to date and reflects roles and responsibilities.	☐	☐	☐
2. Training provided for beginner to advanced CROs is matched to task criticality, complexity, frequency of task performance and competencies required per development stage.	☐	☐	☐

Table C.6: – Training (continued)

Example criteria statement	Yes	To some extent	No
3. A variety of appropriate training methods is used to develop and maintain competence of beginner to advanced CROs. This might include NVQs, scenario based learning, e-learning, and toolbox talks etc.	☐	☐	☐
4. Principles of adult learning are used to help guide the development and delivery of training provided to beginner to advanced CROs.	☐	☐	☐
5. Those responsible for the development and delivery of training provided to beginner to advanced CROs are suitably trained, qualified and periodically reassessed.	☐	☐	☐
6. Changes that affect beginner to advanced CRO training are identified with updates to training undertaken as required.	☐	☐	☐

Table C.7: – Assessment of competence

Example criteria statement	Yes	To some extent	No
1. Assessment plans exist for beginner to advanced CROs and cover, for example, type of assessment, competencies to be assessed, expected performance standard, duration of assessment, frequency of reassessment.	☐	☐	☐
2. Beginner to advanced CRO assessments cover all procedures and processes that are relevant to safety-critical tasks.	☐	☐	☐
3. Beginner to advanced CRO assessments cover all required knowledge and skill for safety-critical task completion.	☐	☐	☐
4. Beginner to advanced CRO assessment methods are appropriate to the safety-critical task and competence requirements of CROs.	☐	☐	☐
5. A range of assessment approaches is used.	☐	☐	☐
6. Beginner to advanced CRO assessments are guided by measurable statements of performance and relevant technical and non-technical knowledge and skill markers.	☐	☐	☐
7. Assessors are appropriately experienced, knowledgeable and have sufficient practical understanding to be credible.	☐	☐	☐
8. Frequency of reassessment is matched to the frequency, complexity and safety criticality of CRO tasks.	☐	☐	☐
9. Safety audits and other performance data are used to help provide evidence of CRO competence.	☐	☐	☐

Table C.7: – Assessment of competence (continued)

Example criteria statement	Yes	To some extent	No
10. There are arrangements in place for managing CROs deemed not competent. For example, retraining, and increased supervision.	☐	☐	☐
11. Changes that affect beginner to advanced CRO assessments are identified, with amendments undertaken as required.	☐	☐	☐

Table C.8: – Review of competence management arrangements

Example criteria statement	Yes	To some extent	No
1. Review of CRO competence management arrangements is carried out against clearly defined criteria.	☐	☐	☐
2. The frequency of reviews is risk based, using risk based triggers and targets identifying areas of weakness with greater frequency.	☐	☐	☐
3. Reviews are conducted using a range of methods and evidence.	☐	☐	☐
4. CROs, their line managers, trainers and assessors as well as other relevant managers are involved in review.	☐	☐	☐
5. Reviewers are appropriately trained and qualified.	☐	☐	☐
6. Opportunities to learn from accidents, incidents, injuries and near misses are taken to make CRO competence management arrangements more effective.	☐	☐	☐
7. Review findings and recommendations are fed back leading to systematic and regular updating and improvement of CRO competence management arrangements.	☐	☐	☐
8. Arrangements are in place for monitoring changes and the effect these could have on review criteria, frequency, methods, with amendments undertaken as required.	☐	☐	☐

ANNEX D
JOB AIDS AND CHECKLISTS

This annex contains job aids and checklists, for:
a)   Utilising national and international CRO standards and regulations.
b)   Using two job analysis techniques – 'critical incident' and 'repertory grid'. Both of these may be of particular interest for:
   –   Managers and supervisors of CROs.
   –   Relevant members of training, human resources, learning and development, talent management functions, for example, those responsible for CRO training and assessment.
c)   Incorporating principles of adult learning into training. This may be of particular interest for relevant members of training, human resources, learning and development, talent management functions, for example, those responsible for CRO training and assessment.
d)   Guiding CRO competence assessments. This may be of particular interest for:
   –   Managers and supervisors of CROs.
   –   Relevant members of training, human resources, learning and development, talent management functions, for example, those responsible for CRO training and assessment.

D.1   CHECKLIST FOR USING CRO STANDARDS AND REGULATIONS

Table D.1: Checklist for using CRO standards and regulations

Key steps and questions	Yes	No
Key step 1: Describe your CRO competence requirement		
Have you identified:		
1. Task types to be considered?	☐	☐
2. Safety-critical tasks for each task type?	☐	☐
3. The complexity of the tasks and frequency of task completion?	☐	☐
4. All relevant knowledge?	☐	☐
5. All relevant technical and non-technical skills?	☐	☐
6. Generic knowledge and skills?	☐	☐
7. Site-specific knowledge and skills?	☐	☐
8. Task type-specific knowledge and skills?	☐	☐
9. Competence requirements per CRO development stage (beginner to advanced)?	☐	☐
10. Have you used multiple sources of information?	☐	☐

Table D.1: Checklist for using CRO standards and regulations (continued)

Key step 2: Map CRO requirements and identify the additional areas		
Have you:		
1. Compared your CRO competence requirements against activities, requirements, knowledge and skills described in the standard and/or regulation?	☐	☐
Key steps and questions	**Yes**	**No**
2. Determined the relevance of standard and/or regulation?	☐	☐
3. Determined which areas can be removed (if applicable)?	☐	☐
4. Identified additional modules/elements?	☐	☐
5. Identified which modules/elements need amending/adjusting (if applicable)?	☐	☐
6. Populated the standard/regulation with plant- and site-specific CRO knowledge, technical and non-technical skills?	☐	☐
7. Populated new modules/elements with plant- and site-specific CRO knowledge, technical and non-technical skills?	☐	☐
8. Used short clear statements?	☐	☐
9. Reviewed and validated the additional modules/elements you have created?	☐	☐
10. Involved CROs and their supervisors in this review/validation?	☐	☐
Key Step 3: Implement standard and/or regulation		
Have you:		
1. Identified how the standard and/or regulation, coupled with any additional modules/elements, will be incorporated into your existing training and assessment programmes?	☐	☐
2. Identified a range of training and assessment methods to achieve this?	☐	☐
3. Identified any additional competencies the trainers and assessors require?	☐	☐
4. Determined the type and frequency of ongoing training and assessment?	☐	☐
5. Organised line manager/CRO discussions to support implementation?	☐	☐
6. Determined the process for review, including sources and indicators?	☐	☐

D.2 CRITICAL INCIDENT TECHNIQUE (DETERMINING COMPETENCIES)

D.2.1 Purpose of critical incident technique

Critical incident technique (CIT) helps in understanding the activities CROs undertake and the competencies required to undertake those activities successfully and to the standard required.

Table D.2: Critical incident analysis steps for determining competencies

Key steps	Overview
Step 1: Identify CRO activities	Confirm activities and tasks you wish to explore.
Step 2: Identify data sources	Identify multiple sources of information, e.g. – CROs to interview – include different grades of CRO to help identify how competence requirements differ by CRO grade. – CRO supervisors to interview – this will provide a perspective on the expected competencies and the level of performance required. – Incident/accident and near miss reports.
Step 3: Collect data	Remember for each activity you are looking to identify: 1. Knowledge and technical and non-technical skills (generic and plant/site-specific). 2. How these differ between CRO development stages, if relevant. When carrying out CRO CIT interviews, ask activity-specific open questions. These could include: **1. Tell me about a time when you carried out (insert activity/task) particularly well.** – What made the situation successful for you? – What exactly did you do and why was it effective? – What were the outcomes? – Would you approach the situation differently in the future, and how? **2. Give me a real example of how not to complete this task/activity?** – What exactly did you do and why was it ineffective? – What were the consequences? – What could you have done differently? **3. Tell me about a time when this (insert activity/task) is most important?** – What was the situation? – Why was the activity so important? – What did you do to ensure it was successfully achieved? – What was the outcome? – What are the consequences if not achieved? When interviewing supervisors use questions such as: 1. Tell me about a time when one of your CROs carried out (insert activity/task) particularly well? 2. Give me a real example of when one of your CROs did not complete this activity/task to the standard required? 3. Can you tell me about a time when this (insert activity/task) is most important?

Table D.2: Critical incident analysis steps for determining competencies (continued)

Key steps	Overview
	When reviewing incident/accident and near miss reports consider the following: – What was the situation? – What technical and non-technical skills were exhibited? – What knowledge was required? – What were the outcomes and why? – What could have been done differently? (What skill and knowledge should have been exhibited/applied?)
Step 4: Represent data	Construct a table to represent the information you have gathered. e.g. {table below} Use short, clear statements for each.
Step 5: Validate data	Present table to all individuals you have interviewed as well as a few subject matter specialists within your organisation for review. Amend as required. You may also wish to ask them to rank the importance of each knowledge and skill.

Activity/ task	Knowledge required	Technical and non-technical skills required	Requirements for CRO grades

D.3 REPERTORY GRID (DETERMINING COMPETENCIES)

D.3.1 Purpose of repertory grid

Repertory grid ('rep grid') is an approach used to help in understanding the competencies required to undertake CRO tasks successfully and to the standard required.

Table D.3: Repertory grid for determining competencies

Key steps	Overview
Step 1: Identify participants for rep grid interviews	Identify multiple participants, e.g. – CROs – include beginner to advanced CROs to help identify how competence requirements differ by CRO development stage. – CRO supervisors and other managers to interview – this will provide a perspective on the expected competencies and the level of performance required.

Table D.3: Repertory grid for determining competencies (continued)

Key steps	Overview
Step 2 Compete rep grid interview	Rep grid interviews are ideally completed with one person at a time, but can be completed with up to three people at a time. Complete the following steps: 1. Ask the interviewee(s) to list out the main activities completed by CROs (up to 10 activities). 2. List each activity on a separate piece of card. 3. Shuffle the cards and ask the interviewee(s) to select three cards. 4. Ask the following question: 'Tell me in what way are the skills needed for two of these activities similar to each other and different from the third?' You should look to gather a clear, relevant, and specific reason for the differences and similarities. 5. Record all similarities and differences. 6. Repeat steps 3 to 5 until all activities have been compared. Ask the interviewee(s) to go through all similarities and differences and rank them in terms of how important they are for successful performance. A one to five scale can be used, e.g. one = not important, five = skill is essential.
Step 3: Represent data	1. Remove all similarities and differences that were commonly ranked as being 'not important'. 2. Construct a table to represent the information you have gathered. e.g. <table><tr><td>Activity</td><td>Knowledge (Ranked order)</td><td>Technical and non-technical skills (Ranked order)</td></tr><tr><td></td><td>1. ......</td><td>1. ......</td></tr><tr><td></td><td>2. ......</td><td>2. ......</td></tr></table> 3. Having constructed this table, see if you can group together knowledge and skills. Provide each grouping with a title, for example process control, decision making, or diligence to safety. Identify how these differ between beginner to advanced CROs, if relevant.
Step 4: Validate data	Present table to all individuals you have interviewed as well as a few subject matter specialists within your organisation for review. Amend as required.

D.4   PRINCIPLES OF ADULT LEARNING

Table D.4: Principles of adult learning

Principles	Remember
1. Motivation	To motivate CROs consider the following: – Select training based on identified training needs, task criticality and the specific competencies you wish to develop. – Foster individual responsibility for learning and ongoing development. – Build rapport with CROs, encourage them to ask open questions and provide constructive and targeted feedback.
2. Experience	To integrate the skills and knowledge into a CRO's current experiences, consider: – Highlighting how the training will help build on and enhance the existing knowledge/skill of CROs. – Providing CROs with the opportunity to apply their existing knowledge and experience. – Providing CROs with reflective learning opportunities, including peer feedback.
3. Learn by doing	CROs learn by doing. To support this: – Set activities within a context that a CRO can relate to. – Focus them on helping CROs tackle/solve problems that they commonly face. – Maximise training and development opportunities outside the classroom. – Use different training methods, materials and approaches matched to training needs. – Match them to the characteristics of the task and operational mode.
4. Respect and trust	CROs will learn better if they are respected and trust their trainers. To help develop respect: – Take an interest in CROs' questions, thoughts and feedback. – Encourage CROs to express ideas, reasoning for thoughts and decisions. – Provide constructive feedback at every opportunity during CRO training. Trainers should be competent and have: – Training skills to facilitate required knowledge and skill. – Assessment skills to conduct formal and informal assessments. – Managerial skills to manage training events and trainees. – Coaching skills to coach CROs not just instruct. – Detailed knowledge of the skills and knowledge CROs require.
5. Feedback	CROs require feedback to learn. Feedback should be: – Specific and objective. – Focused on strengths and areas for development. – Structured around technical and non-technical markers. – Provided by trainers and peers and in different forms.

D.5   CHECKLIST FOR CRO COMPETENCE ASSESSMENT

Table D.5: Checklist for CRO competence assessment

Checklist questions	Yes	No
Do you:		
1. Assess competence across routine, infrequent, abnormal and emergency response conditions?	☐	☐
2. Have 'competent', 'expert' and 'proficient' performance categories?	☐	☐
3. Use a range of assessments to ensure sufficient evidence is gathered to make accurate judgements of competence?	☐	☐
4. Consider, when selecting assessments, task criticality and complexity, frequency of performance, CRO development stage and whether you are assessing knowledge, skills or both?	☐	☐
5. Ensure your assessments are reliable, valid, authentic and fair?	☐	☐
6. Base judgements of competence on robust evidence, gathered from a number of assessments?	☐	☐
7. Use multiple assessors to make judgements of competence?	☐	☐
8. Have 'pass/fail' criteria for elements/areas of assessments that are considered 'critical'?	☐	☐
9. Record judgements of competence and create CRO competence portfolios?	☐	☐
10. Have a system for CROs deemed 'not competent'?	☐	☐
11. Develop and assess assessment, managerial and coaching skills of your assessors?	☐	☐
12. Develop and assess the relevant knowledge, technical and non-technical CRO skills of your assessors?	☐	☐
13. Provide ongoing training and assessment for your assessors?	☐	☐
14. Communicate assessment results to CROs, line managers and trainers?	☐	☐
15. Look at assessment results across CROs to help identify if there is a common competence deficiency?	☐	☐

ANNEX E
ROUTINE TASKS: EXAMPLE COMPETENCIES, TRAINING AND ASSESSMENTS

Table E.1: Example CRO knowledge, technical and non-technical skills, training needs and sources of information for routine tasks

	Description
Example knowledge	Control room systems, their function, connectivity, tolerance and capacity to monitor and maintain normal operating conditions.
	Plant layout and connective systems relevant to control room operations.
	Plant conditions, processes, operating capacity and tolerance during normal operations.
	Composition and properties of product and chemicals during normal operating conditions.
	Major accident hazards being controlled by engineering, process and production risk controls relevant to routine CRO tasks.
	Safe systems of work and operating procedures for routine CRO tasks.
Example technical skills	Physical operation of control room controls and devices to access system status information and relevant schematics.
	Physical operation of control room controls and devices to maintain product flows, temperatures etc. within normal operating limits.
	Writing permits to work and recording relevant control room operational information during shift, handover and administration.
Example non-technical skills	Monitoring and interpreting control room process information to maintain situational awareness during completion of routine control room tasks.
	Prioritisation of control room process information and decision making during completion of routine control room tasks.
	Communications within and outside control room during routine tasks.
	Team working and compliance with procedures.
Example training needs	Plant design, functioning and production process cycle.
	The role of control room operations in plant functioning and production process, including functioning capability and limits.
	Basic engineering and basic chemical engineering.
	Control room devices and controls for routine tasks.
	Safe systems of work, normal operating procedures, health and safety management and quality management for routine control room activity.
	Major accident hazards being controlled during routine control room operations and the engineering systems and processes in place to control these risks.

Table E.1: Example CRO knowledge, technical and non-technical skills, training needs and sources of information for routine tasks (continued)

	Description
	Mandatory requirements under regulations such as COMAH, Health and Safety Act, Working Time Directive etc. for routine control room operator tasks.
	Relevant non-technical skills training for routine control room tasks such as CRM and safety behaviour awareness training.
Sources of information	Structured observations, talk/walk-through of routine task completion in live control room.
	Knowledge, technical and non-technical skills review of operating procedures and safe systems of work for routine control room tasks.
	Statutory regulations such as COMAH and NOSs (Cogent and OPITO) relevant to technical skills/knowledge for routine CRO tasks.
	On-the-job performance data of CROs completing routine tasks.
	Peer review based on IOSH process.

Table E.2: Example training approaches for routine tasks

	Example training methods	**Main advantages**	**Main disadvantages**
Knowledge	**Interactive classroom based training.** Methods can include: – presentations of knowledge and key concepts and theories; – models and diagrams to explain plant functioning, processes, engineering system etc, and – case studies, pictures and videos, including hazard spotting activities.	Interactive learning can 'bring the topic area to life'. Provides a learning environment for CRO to ask questions away from the workplace.	Can be artificial as it is based in the classroom. CROs may feel uncomfortable being in a classroom.

Table E.2: Example training approaches for routine tasks (continued)

	Example training methods	Main advantages	Main disadvantages
	Structured on-the-job training and job rotation to develop and apply knowledge. This should include on-the-job training and job rotation within and outside of the control room.	Fosters familiarisation with plant operations. CROs are likely to feel more comfortable. Provides 'live' observation and interaction with plant.	Job rotation opportunities can be limited due to staff numbers and available people to coach. On-the-job training can be unstructured and hard to monitor effectiveness.
	Toolbox talks, shift meetings and handovers.	Provides opportunity to share knowledge and information across the team. Can be focused on specific and relevant operational issues. Can be used as an opportunity to reinforce and refresh knowledge.	Difficult to monitor learning. Requires very effective facilitation and coaching.
	Involvement in health and safety committees, other initiatives etc.	Can help CRO develop a better understanding of safe systems of work, procedures etc.	Level of workforce involvement in HSEQ may not be sufficient for CROs' development. CROs may not have the time to be involved.
Technical skill	**Supervised instruction and practice allowing CROs to perform the technical skills required for routine control room operations, under supervision.**	Provides a 'live' environment to practise skills and receive feedback on performance. Can provide opportunity to further develop knowledge, if trainer uses talk/walk-through approach.	Needs dedicated time within the shift to provide supervised instruction.

Table E.2: Example training approaches for routine tasks (continued)

	Example training methods	Main advantages	Main disadvantages
Non-technical skill	**CROs carrying out 'live' routine tasks under supervision, with a focus on ensuring non-technical skills are developed and demonstrated.** This can include cognitive talk/walk-throughs of non-technical skills being applied and why.	Provides the 'hands on' learning in a 'live' environment. Keeps CROs on operating duty and can provide further development and demonstration of non-technical knowledge.	Danger of 'poor/bad' habits being taught. May be difficult to find the time and opportunity to carry out these talk/walk-throughs. CROs may feel under pressure within the 'live' environment.
	Non-technical skill scenarios for routine control room tasks. CROs practise non-technical skills in process simulator and/or simulated environment. Simulated environment could consist of role-play scenarios using pictures or computers with mock-up control room information presented.	Provides dedicated practice in safe environment, with peer feedback. Process simulators or simulated environments can be targeted towards certain topics for refresher training.	CROs can challenge the realism of mock-ups and scenarios. Mock-ups and simulators can make CROs feel uncomfortable. Process simulators, if used, can be very expensive.

Table E.3: Example assessment approaches for routine tasks

	Example assessment methods	Main advantages	Main disadvantages
Knowledge	**Written tests:** – Multiple choice written tests to assess knowledge required for routine control room tasks. – Work based multiple choice tests, based on work place examples of routine control room activities/situations.	Multiple choice questions can be standardised. Easy to administer.	Probability that CRO can guess question answers. Relies on CROs' ability to write and construct written material.

Table E.3: Example assessment approaches for routine tasks (continued)

	Example assessment methods	Main advantages	Main disadvantages
	On-the-job talk/walk-throughs.	Obtained firsthand evidence of knowledge. CROs may be more comfortable with this type of assessment.	Relies on questioning skills of assessors. Must be combined with skill assessments to make judgements of competence.
Technical skill	**Technical skill focused observations:** – On-the-job observation of CROs carrying out routine control room tasks. – Remote observations. If possible using CCTV, voice tapes etc. to observe technical skills being applied during routine control room operations. – Process simulator observations.	Provides high quality evidence of application of technical skill for routine tasks. Assessments can be undertaken as part of line manager's job. This can be combined with the non-technical skills cognitive walk-through.	Can be distracting to CROs. CROs may behave differently under observation.
Non-technical skill	**Routine control room task cognitive talk/walk-through.** This can include 'what if' questions to understand how the CRO would apply skills and knowledge in different circumstances/situations within the control room. Assessments can be carried out in the control room or within a process simulator/ simulated environment.	Flexible approach that can be used to assess knowledge and skill. Raises self-awareness of the CRO taking part in the assessment.	CROs may find it difficult to carry out tasks and talk through simultaneously. CROs may find it too difficult to articulate some non-technical skills.

Table E.3: Example assessment approaches for routine tasks (continued)

	Example assessment methods	Main advantages	Main disadvantages
	Review of work performance. This might include: – Review of documents produced as part of routine task completion such as permits to work, handover, reports and operational logs. – Review of job performance data, for example, meeting performance and safety targets etc. – Supervisors and peer feedback. – CRO feedback interview.	Data are readily available for review.	Causes of poor or good performance are inferred. Data need to be supplemented with observations and talkthroughs.
	Self-directed peer assessments. CROs are assessed by their peers completing routine tasks within the control room.	Peer assessment can help enhance performance.	Peers must receive detailed training to be able to carry out assessment.
	CRO team assessment during routine control room tasks.	Provides an assessment of team competence.	Can be difficult to assess the CRO team together.

ANNEX F
INFREQUENT TASKS: EXAMPLE COMPETENCIES, TRAINING AND ASSESSMENTS

Table F.1: Example CRO knowledge, technical and non-technical skills, training needs and sources of information for infrequent tasks

	Description
Example knowledge	Expected operating capacity, product pressure flows, temperatures, tolerance and limits etc. during infrequent control room tasks.
	Connectivity and dependency of relevant engineering systems and processes during infrequent control room tasks, such as isolation and testing of assets and equipment.
	Major accident hazards during infrequent control room tasks, and relevant engineering, process and production risk controls.
	Specific safe systems of work and operating procedures for completing infrequent control room tasks.
	Specific handover, communication and reporting requirements for infrequent control room tasks such as plant shut-down, critical equipment isolation for testing.
Example technical skill	Physical operation of controls and devices to access system status information and relevant schematics during infrequent control room tasks.
	Physical activation of alarms if normal operating limits are breached during infrequent control room tasks.
Example non-technical skill	Detecting and recognising patterns, trends and abnormalities in process during infrequent tasks.
	Communicating safety-critical information during infrequent tasks, within and outside control room, and across handover.
Example training needs	Plant, asset and equipment behaviour and functioning during infrequent control room tasks, for example rapid cooling of assets during shut-down and the major accident hazards being controlled during these operations.
	Relevant engineering process and safe systems of work to complete infrequent control room tasks and the role/responsibility of control room operations and CRO in maintaining normal operating capacity during these tasks.
	Relevant non-technical skills training for infrequent control room tasks such as maintaining global awareness and prioritisation.

Table F.1: Example CRO knowledge, technical and non-technical skills, training needs and sources of information for infrequent tasks (continued)

	Description
Sources of information	Structured observations and talk/walk-through of infrequent task completion in live control room, if possible, or process simulator/ simulated scenario.
	Critical incident review of records, and reports of previous completion of infrequent control room tasks, for example previous shut-downs, equipment and component isolation.
	Safety case requirements for CROs and control room operations to maintain normal operating limits during infrequent task completion.
	Job analysis interviews (CROs, supervisors, safety department etc.) focused on completion of infrequent control room tasks.
	Statutory regulations such as COMAH and NOSs (Cogent and OPITO) relevant to technical skills/knowledge for infrequent CRO tasks.

Table F.2: Example training approaches for infrequent tasks

	Example training methods	Main advantages	Main disadvantages
Knowledge	**Infrequent task classroom based training.** This might include: – interactive presentations, and – use of videos and example case studies to carry out hazard/ error spotting activities.	CROs may not have completed infrequent tasks and hence the interactive learning creates greater realism. Videos and interactive presentations can be used for ongoing refresher training, particularly during briefings and toolbox talks.	Is still an artificial environment. Must be supported by scenario based hands-on learning.
	Structured job rotation. Across plant and within the control room, to develop knowledge of plant operations and functioning relevant to infrequent control room tasks. This might include maintenance activity, such as isolations of equipment and testing.	Helps develop understanding of how control room tasks affect infrequent operations and help control major accident hazards.	Likely to be limited observation of 'live' infrequent tasks being completed.

Table F.2: Example training approaches for infrequent tasks (continued)

	Example training methods	Main advantages	Main disadvantages
	Interactive toolbox talks. Using videos, pictures and case studies to demonstrate plant, asset and equipment behaviour and functioning during infrequent control room tasks.	Provides interactive ongoing refresher training. Can be used as impromptu training, i.e. delivered before CROs are required to complete an infrequent task.	Reliant on coaching and facilitation skills of the trainer/ supervisor. Can take time to deliver this type of toolbox talk and hence requires careful time management.
Technical skill	**Infrequent tasks process simulation.** – Supervised instruction and practice allowing CROs to perform the technical skills required for infrequent control room tasks. Carried out under supervision within a control room simulated environment or process simulator. – Can include observation of experienced CROs carrying out infrequent control room tasks within a simulated environment or process simulator.	Provides a realistic environment to practise skills and receive feedback on performance. Provides demonstration of technical skill within a realistic environment.	May be very few technical skills required for the CRO role. This training should be combined with non-technical skill observations/ talk/walk-throughs. Simulators can be very expensive.
Non-technical skills	**Operational debriefs with CROs after infrequent task completion.**	Provides contextual learning. Can help develop/ refresh skills and knowledge.	Can become 'blame' exercises. Requires careful structuring and facilitation.

Table F.2: Example training approaches for infrequent tasks (continued)

	Example training methods	Main advantages	Main disadvantages
	Showcase observations. Observations of infrequent tasks being completed on other sites, or by other organisations.	Provides opportunity to observe infrequent tasks being completed. Helps develop knowledge and skill.	Requires significant planning and can be resource intensive. Other organisations may have different operating procedures, working practices and equipment.
	Non-technical skill scenarios for infrequent control room tasks. CROs practise non-technical skills in process simulator and/or simulated environment. Role plays and computer screen mock-ups could be used to create a more 'realistic environment' for practice.	Provides opportunity to practise a range of infrequent tasks in safe environment with peer feedback. Simulations and simulator scenarios can be targeted to the CROs' key areas for development. Simulations or simulated environments can be used for refresher training.	Mock-ups and simulators can make CROs feel uncomfortable or nervous. Simulators can be very expensive. CROs may behave differently in a mock-up and role play environment.
	Planned infrequent task completion. Planned shut-downs, equipment isolation and testing etc, provide the opportunity for CROs to complete infrequent CRO tasks under supervision.	Provides the 'hands on' practice. Helps CROs understand how to behave in a 'real' environment completing infrequent tasks.	CROs may feel under pressure within the 'live' environment. May be very limited opportunity to carry out this form of training.

Table F.3: Example assessment approaches for infrequent tasks

	Example assessment methods	Main advantages	Main disadvantages
Knowledge	**Scenario based multiple choice questions.** Different infrequent tasks are described, such as plant shut-down, isolation of equipment etc, with relevant multiple choice questions.	Provides standardised form of testing. Focuses on applying knowledge.	Probability that CRO can guess question answers.
	Knowledge video assessment. Short videos of infrequent tasks being completed with relevant knowledge questions.	Provides an interactive form of assessment.	Can be expensive to develop the videos.
Technical skill	**Infrequent task simulator/simulated technical skills assessment.**	Provides realistic environment. Can be combined with non-technical skill assessment.	Still an artificial environment and CROs may behave differently.
Non-technical skills	**Assessment of planned infrequent task completion.**	Provides real life assessment of performance. Can include technical skill assessment.	May be very limited opportunity to carry out this form of assessment. Must ensure that this form of assessment does not distract the CRO.
	Process simulator/ simulated assessment of infrequent control room task completion. This can include non-technical skill observation and cognitive talk/walk-through assessment.	Should be combined with technical skill assessment. Opportunity to gather evidence from the CRO and peers.	May require multiple assessors if assessing knowledge, technical and non-technical skill.

ANNEX G
ABNORMAL TASKS: EXAMPLE COMPETENCIES, TRAINING AND ASSESSMENTS

Table G.1: Example CRO knowledge, technical and non-technical skills, training needs and sources of information for abnormal tasks

	Description
Example knowledge	Causes of abnormal conditions and the effect these have on the stability of products and process and asset integrity.
	Plant layout and the potential 'knock-on' effects of abnormal conditions on other connecting complex systems/processes.
	Major accident hazards relating to abnormal conditions and the engineering processes and systems in place to help restore operations.
	Critical screens, devices, readings, performance data, etc, to navigate and monitor within the control room to detect and diagnose abnormal/upset condition.
	Relevant control room schematics, drawings to access and the process for interpreting these drawings to inform diagnosis and response decisions.
	Principles of effective safety-critical communication and risk based decision making and prioritisation within the control room during abnormal/upset conditions.
Example technical skills	Physical operation of controls and devices to access system status, schematics and drawings etc. to diagnose abnormal/upset condition and restore operations to 'normal'.
	Recording relevant operational information during abnormal conditions and after restoration.
Example non-technical skills	Risk based prioritisation of information to develop and implement response plan to restore operations to 'normal'.
	Ongoing navigation, interpretation and monitoring of critical information to understand impact of response and maintain overview of plant/process/equipment functioning.
	Maintaining situational awareness of other connected complex systems/processes that may be affected by localised abnormal conditions.
	Coordination of response within the control room and to selected field operator personnel.

Table G.1: Example CRO knowledge, technical and non-technical skills, training needs and sources of information for abnormal tasks (continued)

	Description
Example training needs	Definition of what constitutes abnormal conditions and the safe systems of work and operating procedures to be followed.
	Role/responsibility of control room operator during abnormal/upset conditions.
	Product/chemical reactions taking place during abnormal conditions and the potential changes to the stability and properties of chemicals and products.
	Plant, asset and equipment behaviour and functioning during abnormal conditions and the potential changes in stability and integrity.
	Relevant non-technical skills training for abnormal conditions such as risk based communication, challenge and verification of information to maintain situational awareness, risk based prioritisation and decision making, detecting and diagnosing faults.
	Human factors in abnormal conditions.
Sources of information	Structured observation and talk/walk-through of control room operators completing abnormal condition tasks in process simulator/simulated scenario.
	Job analysis interviews (CROs, supervisors, safety department etc.) focused on completion of control room abnormal condition tasks, including critical incident review of previous abnormal conditions, focusing on CROs.
	NOSs (Cogent and OPITO), relevant to CRO for detecting, diagnosing and responding to abnormal conditions.
	Safety case requirements for CROs and control room operations during abnormal conditions. This can include HAZOPS and human HAZOPS, fault trees and risk assessments.

Table G.2: Example training approaches for abnormal tasks

	Example training methods	Main advantages	Main disadvantages
Knowledge	**Practical based training using models, diagrams and videos illustrating the causes of abnormal conditions and their effects.**	Creates greater realism and allows CROs to ask questions and explore content. Videos and interactive presentations can be used for ongoing refresher training.	Must be supported by 'scenario based' hands-on learning.

Table G.2: Example training approaches for abnormal tasks (continued)

	Example training methods	Main advantages	Main disadvantages
	Abnormal event analysis to illustrate the causes of abnormal conditions and their effects on products and process.	Provides up to date examples to work through. Can be used to structure toolbox talks and refresher training.	Reliant on coaching and facilitation skills of the trainer/ supervisor. Needs up to date examples.
	HAZOPS and risk assessments. Involve CROs in relevant safety case HAZOPS, including human HAZOPS and risks assessments.	Can help CROs understand engineering systems, process, procedures and safe systems of work.	CROs may need additional training to understand the HAZOPS and risk assessment process.
Technical skill	**Fault condition technical skills training.** This should cover, using process simulator or simulated environment, a range of fault conditions as well as multiple fault conditions. This can be supported by observing the technical skills of experienced CROs completing abnormal CRO tasks.	Allows CROs to perform the technical skills required for abnormal control room tasks under supervision. Provides opportunity for CROs to see their peers demonstrate technical skills.	Still an artificial environment. Difficult to replicate other competing pressures during abnormal conditions.
Non-technical skills	**Impromptu non-technical skills briefings/ toolbox talks for process upset/abnormal conditions.** These should also draw on incidents and lessons learnt from other industries.	Can target toolbox talks that are delivered after abnormal/upset condition. Provides interactive refresher training.	Can be sensitive issues that need to be addressed before toolbox talks are delivered.

Table G.2: Example training approaches for abnormal tasks (continued)

	Example training methods	Main advantages	Main disadvantages
	Fault conditions, as well as multiple fault conditions, non-technical skills training. This can include: – Interactive classroom training, with case studies and videos. – 'Live' observation during simulator/ simulation activity and/ or a recording played to CROs. – Practice in process simulator and/or simulated environment.	Provides opportunity to practise different fault sequences in a safe environment with peer and trainer feedback. Simulations or simulated environments can be used for refresher training.	Mock-ups and simulators can make CROs feel uncomfortable or nervous. Simulating the changing nature and multiple demands of abnormal conditions can be challenging.
	Self-directed learning. This can include: – Individual and group assignments. – Abnormal condition one-to-one peer coaching and feedback. Particularly useful in helping CROs reflect on their performance when they have been involved in abnormal conditions.	Creates responsibility and motivation for learning. Assignments can be used as refresher training exercises. Fosters informal learning.	CROs may find it difficult to take control of their learning. Can be hard to monitor effectiveness.

Table G.3: Example assessment approaches for abnormal tasks

	Example assessment methods	Main advantages	Main disadvantages
Knowledge	**Fault sequence assessment.** CRO presented with a range of different fault sequences and asked knowledge based questions. This can be a written test, a multiple choice question set or an oral test.	Oral test does not require the CRO to articulate answers in writing. Focuses on applying knowledge.	Oral test relies on CRO ability to articulate answers verbally. Written test relies on CRO ability to articulate answers in writing.

Table G.3: Example assessment approaches for abnormal tasks (continued)

	Example assessment methods	Main advantages	Main disadvantages
	On-the-job abnormal condition technical assessment. This can include: – knowledge based questions out on site; and – control room based knowledge questions.	CROs may be more comfortable with this type of assessment.	Relies on skill of assessor to ask questions. Must be combined with skill assessments to make judgements of competence.
Technical skill	**Fault condition and multiple fault condition technical skills assessment.** This should assess the full range of fault conditions as well as multiple fault conditions, using process simulator or simulated environment.	Provides realistic environment for skill assessment. Can be combined with non-technical skills assessment.	Can be difficult without a simulator to replicate the changing nature of abnormal conditions.
Non-technical skills	**Impromptu abnormal/ process upset condition review assessment.** After a CRO has dealt with an abnormal/process upset condition a review is undertaken to assess how well the CRO performed. It should include a structured cognitive interview talking through the tasks, actions and decisions the CRO took during the upset/abnormal condition.	Based on a real recent event. Can be combined with knowledge and technical skill assessment.	CROs may find it hard to recall all actions and decisions they undertook during the abnormal condition. Does not provide the assessor with direct observation of CRO performance.
	Fault condition and multiple fault condition non-technical skills assessment. CROs undertake abnormal condition tasks to detect, diagnose and rectify fault and multiple fault scenarios within a simulated or process simulator environment. This can include a cognitive talk/walk-through.	Provides high quality evidence. Assesses multiple fault conditions in a changing operating environment.	Still an artificial environment and CROs may perform differently in this environment. Requires time and resource to create simulated environment.

Table G.3: Example assessment approaches for abnormal tasks (continued)

	Example assessment methods	Main advantages	Main disadvantages
	Psychometric testing, assessing cognitive abilities required for abnormal/upset condition CRO tasks, e.g: – numerical reasoning; – verbal reasoning, and – inductive and deductive reasoning.	Quick and easy to apply. Good predictor of job performance.	Does not provide evidence of actual job performance. Needs specific certification and level of competence to administer and analyse test results.
	Fault condition and multiple fault condition team based assessment.	Provides an assessment of team competence.	Can be difficult to observe the CRO team working together during an assessment.

ANNEX H
EMERGENCY RESPONSE TASKS: EXAMPLE COMPETENCIES, TRAINING AND ASSESSMENTS

Table H.1: Example CRO knowledge, technical and non-technical skills, training needs and sources of information for emergency response tasks

	Description
Example knowledge	Causes of critical events and emergencies and what these mean for the stability of products and process, integrity of assets and control of major accident hazards.
	Critical emergency systems such as fire and gas control systems and EDS, including operation and implication of their operation.
	Implications of significant loss of process control, fire or gas release, or significant loss of containment on employee and public safety, environment and plant/asset integrity.
	Control room systems and their functions to support the detection, diagnosis and coordination of critical situations/ emergencies as well as operate emergency response systems such as activation of emergency plant shut-down or critical asset isolation.
	Emergency response procedures that should be followed in the control room during emergency response.
Example technical skill	Physical operation of controls and devices to access system status, schematics and drawings etc. to diagnose critical/ emergency situation.
	Physical operation of controls and devices to operate critical emergency systems.
	Recording relevant operational information during critical/ emergency situation.
Example non-technical skill	Willingness to respond to emergencies.
	Dynamic risk assessment, decision making and prioritisation of information to take action.
	Clear and timely safety-critical communications to relevant line managers and other personnel.
	Leading and instructing to coordinate response within the control room and to selected field operators.
	Reviewing effectiveness of emergency response actions and maintaining dynamic situational awareness through ongoing navigation, interpretation and monitoring of critical information.
	Working with and supporting multi agency and gold command responses to emergency events.

Table H.1: Example CRO knowledge, technical and non-technical skills, training needs and sources of information for emergency response tasks (continued)

	Description
Example training needs	Critical conditions and the characteristics of an emergency.
	Product/chemical reactions taking place during critical situations and the plant, asset and equipment behaviour and functioning during such conditions.
	The effects loss of containment or fire can have on the properties and stability of products and/or chemicals, including how these chemicals and products behave, for example, when released into the environment.
	Relevant fail-safe engineering processes and systems in place to help manage and mitigate risk in emergency situations.
	Plant-wide emergency response plans and the role and responsibilities of CROs during these emergencies, including whom they communicate and coordinate with.
	Principles of effective emergency response including relevant non-technical skills training for emergency response, such as multitasking in dynamic situations, stress management, staying calm under pressure, making decisions using incomplete information within dynamic situations.
Sources of information	Review of emergency response procedures, critical systems and engineering processes for control room operations.
	Critical incident review of emergency response conditions, across industries.
	NOSs (Cogent and OPITO), relevant to control room operations for controlling critical conditions and responding to emergencies.
	Human reliant/based emergency response claims made on CROs, within the safety case.
	Existing research into CRO competence for supporting emergency response.
	Job analysis interviews (CROs, supervisors, safety department etc.) focused on completion of control room emergency response tasks.

Table H.2: Example training approaches for emergency response tasks

	Example training methods	Main advantages	Main disadvantages
Knowledge	**Dynamic practical based training using models, diagrams and videos.** Focus is on helping CROs understand the dynamic functioning of plant and processes during an emergency response.	Creates greater realism. Videos and interactive presentations can be used for refresher training. Helps CRO understand how the plant is functioning and potential major accident hazards during emergency response.	Must be supported by scenario based hands-on learning. Hard to replicate the dynamic nature of emergency response.
	Specific emergency response case study analysis. Uses recent examples of emergency responses from a range of industries. This can include videos, for example, from the US Chemical Safety Board.	Provides up to date training, as the sessions can be run soon after a new case study example is available. Provides interactive ongoing refresher training.	Needs up to date examples with detailed learning available.
	Emergency response plant orientation training. Focus on helping CROs understand plant layout, potential knock-on effects of critical situations, evacuation procedures and impacts of emergency shut-downs and other emergency critical systems.	Allows CROs to understand the full impact of emergencies and what it means for plant functioning. Provides detailed knowledge of orientation to aid evacuations, etc.	Can be difficult for CROs to really appreciate the scale of risk and impacts relating to emergencies. Scenario learning is required.
	Major accident scenarios safety case analysis. Involve CROs in relevant HAZOPS, including human HAZOPS and risk assessments relating to the process and engineering systems for controlling major accident scenarios.	Can help CROs understand engineering systems, processes, procedures and safe systems of work.	CRO may need additional training to understand the HAZOP and risk assessment process. HAZOPS and risk assessments may be infrequent.

Table H.2: Example training approaches for emergency response tasks (continued)

	Example training methods	Main advantages	Main disadvantages
Technical skill	**Control room emergency response simulated technical skills observations and practice.** This should cover a range of emergencies and critical conditions, including activation of emergency systems and shut-downs.	Provides demonstration of technical skill by qualified CROs. Provides supervised instruction and practice.	Difficult without a simulator to replicate the dynamic nature of abnormal conditions.
Non-technical skills	**Other organisation/ industry emergency response simulations.**	Provides opportunity to observe emergency response drills being conducted.	Need to develop working relationships with other organisations and industries.
	Dynamic non-technical skills training for emergency responses. This might include: – Classroom training - videos, example case studies, group activities etc. – Dynamic emergency response simulation – CROs carrying out process simulator/ simulated emergency response tasks. – Emergency response one- to-one peer coaching and feedback, using a buddy system.	Non-technical skills for dynamic events are better explained and demonstrated through interactive learning. Use of talk/walk-throughs help develop technical and non-technical skills and knowledge.	Reliant on coaching and facilitation skills of the trainers. Can be difficult to replicate the dynamic nature of events.
	Actor-led emergency response scenarios. Actors act out emergency response scenarios. CROs stop and start scenarios, influencing decisions and actions.	Provides active learning. Helps CROs observe different emergency scenarios and explore the impact of decisions and actions.	Can be expensive to use actor training companies. Unlikely to be able to simulate a full scale emergency.

Table H.2: Example training approaches for emergency response tasks (continued)

	Example training methods	Main advantages	Main disadvantages
	Impromptu non-technical skills briefings/toolbox talks for emergency response.	Can be delivered after an emergency has occurred either on an organisation's site or within wider industry.	May take time to gather enough information after an emergency to deliver an effective toolbox talk.
	Plant-wide emergency scenarios and drills. This can be planned or unplanned, involve actors and on occasion involve multi-agency and gold command emergency responses.	Multi-agency and gold command scenarios help the CRO understand the command and control structure in an emergency and how this may affect their decision and actions.	Requires significant resources and planning. Can be difficult to plan and implement a multi-agency emergency scenario.

Table H.3: Example assessment approaches for emergency response tasks

	Example assessment methods	Main advantages	Main disadvantages
Knowledge	**Dynamic scenario based technical assessments.** CROs are presented with an emergency scenario and asked knowledge based questions. The scenarios can be made dynamic by presenting information in a staggered manner so that the CRO has to develop their understanding of the emergency as the assessment progresses.	Provides interactive test of knowledge. Can be provided in a range of forms such as written test, multiple choice test, oral test and include diagrams, videos, pictures and models. Looks to create dynamic nature of emergencies.	Relies on assessors' ability to ask questions and listen effectively to the answers provided by CROs. Can take time to develop dynamic scenarios used for testing.

Table H.3: Example assessment approaches for emergency response tasks (continued)

	Example assessment methods	Main advantages	Main disadvantages
	Emergency response procedural test. Multiple choice question test regarding procedural requirements, protocols and systems of work for emergency response.	Specific test of knowledge relating to emergency response.	Static multiple choice assessment. Should be combined with a more dynamic test.
	Emergency response plant orientation assessment. Site based assessment of CROs' understanding of plant layout, potential knock-on effects of critical situations, evacuation procedures and impacts of emergency shut-downs and other emergency critical systems on process and control of major accident hazards.	Provides another assessment of knowledge.	Focuses on knowledge acquisition rather than application of knowledge.
Technical skill	**Control room emergency response simulated technical skills assessment.** Assessments of specific CRO technical skills required for emergency response. This can be simulated or within a process simulator.	Provides a simulated assessment focused on technical skill which can be combined with non-technical skill assessment.	Difficult, without a simulator, to replicate the dynamic nature of emergency situations.

Table H.3: Example assessment approaches for emergency response tasks (continued)

	Example assessment methods	**Main advantages**	**Main disadvantages**
Non-technical skills	**Dynamic emergency response simulation assessment.** CROs should be assessed undertaking tasks individually and as part of a response team. Scenarios must create dynamic environments with multiple task demands as well as distractions and multiple communications. Simulated environments can use mock-up computer screens presenting major fault sequences, activation of critical alarms, incoming calls of emergencies and process failure etc, with the information changing over time. This assessment can be supported by a non-technical skills cognitive talk/walk-through.	Provides a realistic environment to assess non-technical skills for emergency response. Assesses team performance during emergency response situations. Can be used to assess technical skill as well. Talk/walk-through can include 'what if' questions to understand how the CRO would apply skills and knowledge if different situations arose or different information was presented.	Can be difficult to replicate the dynamic nature of events and is unclear how CROs will react when faced with a real emergency. Relies on assessors' questioning and listening ability, in terms of gathered evidence from CROs and peers. May require multiple assessors.

Table H.3: Example assessment approaches for emergency response tasks (continued)

	Example assessment methods	Main advantages	Main disadvantages
	Plant-wide emergency scenarios and drills. CRO is assessed taking part in the drill. This assessment can include: – Observations of CRO during the drill. – Review of documents produced and any job performance data indicating performance during the scenario/drill. – Feedback from supervisors and peers regarding the CRO's performance during the scenario/drill. – Structured cognitive CRO interview talking through the tasks, actions and decisions the CRO took during the scenario/drill.	Supports the simulated/ simulation assessments. Provides a range of evidence to assess competence of CRO during an emergency response.	Requires significant resources and planning. It will not be possible to carry out these assessments very often. CROs may find the simulation very stressful.
	Psychometric tests Including: – Assessing cognitive abilities required for emergency response tasks e.g.time-critical inductive and deductive reasoning. – Measuring personality characteristics relevant to emergency response, e.g. working under extreme pressure, adapting to dynamic environments.	Quick and easy to apply. Cognitive tests are often a good predictor of job performance.	Does not provide evidence of how a CRO will actually behave in an emergency. Need specific certification and level of competence to administer and analyse the results of such tests.

ANNEX I
CRO TRAINERS AND ASSESSORS: EXAMPLE COMPETENCIES, TRAINING AND ASSESSMENTS

Table I.1: Example knowledge and skill requirements for CRO trainers and assessors

Skills and knowledge	Description for CRO trainers	Description for CRO assessors
Training/ assessing skills	This includes: – presentation skills; – inspirational communication of ideas and concepts; – interaction and interpersonal skills; – providing clear instructions and direction; – clear demonstration of the skills and behaviours expected of CROs; – observation of CROs' performance using technical and non-technical markers; – demonstration of the attitudes and behaviours expected of the organisation, for example, respect, diversity, collaboration; – engaging with trainee CROs; – drawing out and building on CROs' existing knowledge, and – using multiple training methods, such as classroom based training, on-the-job training, scenario and simulated learning.	These include: – providing clear instructions and direction during assessments; – effective administration of assessments such as written tests; – building rapport with the CRO; – interaction and interpersonal skills during assessments; – accurate assessment of CRO's performance using technical and non-technical markers during assessments; – making accurate judgements of competence based on objective evidence, using defined assessment criteria; – using multiple assessment methods, such as observations, written tests, simulation/simulator assessments, cognitive walk-throughs etc, and – using on-the-job performance data and feedback from management and supervisors to inform judgements of competence.

Table I.1: Example knowledge and skill requirements for CRO trainers and assessors (continued)

Skills and knowledge	Description for CRO trainers	Description for CRO assessors
Managerial skills	Effective management of training, including: – dealing with any challenges to trainer authority or content of the training; – time management; – dealing with sensitive issues that have been raised by learners; – adapting training plans to meet the learning requirements of CROs, and – ensuring CROs are provided with a range of different learning opportunities and environments.	Effective management of assessments including: – organising and arranging assessments; – managing time during the assessments and afterwards for feedback; – explaining the purpose of assessments and dealing with any challenges during assessments constructively, and – managing individuals who are being assessed, including stress management, negative emotions and dealing with sensitive issues that may be raised during the assessments.
Coaching skills	Coaching and providing feedback including: – asking open and closed questions, where appropriate; – empathetic listening; – fostering learning environment of self-reflection to increase self-awareness, where relevant; – providing specific, objective and focused feedback to enhance performance, using technical and non-technical markers; – acknowledging good performance and strengths and identifying areas for development; – fostering an environment where the CRO feels comfortable and can perform to the best of their ability, and – providing feedback sensitively and developing clear plans for improvement.	
Knowledge	Detailed understanding and ability to demonstrate the knowledge and skills CROs will require. This is knowledge- and skill-specific to the training/assessment the trainer/assessor will be expected to deliver.	

Table I.2: Example methods for training and assessing CRO trainers and assessors

Method	Description of train the trainer methods	Description of train the assessor methods
Qualifications	Training and coaching qualifications for the role, and the assessments that accompany these qualifications. Example qualifications, with assessments to help develop trainer competence might include: – Level 3 Award in Understanding the Principles and Practice of Learning and Development; – Level 3 Award in Facilitating Learning and Development; – Level 4 Award in Learning and Development; – Level 4 Diploma in Learning and Development; – Level 3 or 4 Award in Preparing to Teach in the Lifelong Learning Sector (PTLLS); – Level 3 or 4 Certificate in Teaching in the Lifelong Learning Sector (CTTLS).	Assessment qualifications. Example qualifications, with assessments to help develop assessor competence might include: – Level 3 Award in Understanding the Principles and Practice of Assessment; – Level 3 Award in Assessing Competence in the Work Environment; – Level 3 Award Assessing Vocationally Related Achievement; – Level 3 Certificate in Assessing Vocational Achievement; – Level 4 Award in Understanding the Internal Quality Assurance of Assessment Processes and Practice; – Level 4 Certificate in Leading the Internal Quality Assurance of Assessment Processes and Practice; – Level 4 Award in the External Quality Assurance of Assessment Processes and Practice.
Participating in CRO training	Provide trainers/assessors with the relevant training and assessments CROs receive. This will develop the trainers'/assessors' knowledge, technical and non-technical skills required for the CRO role, and help them understand the type and content of the training and assessment CROs require.	
Train the trainer/ assessor sessions	Provide trainers/assessors with: – classroom training consisting of engaging presentations and examples to help trainers/assessors, and – opportunities to deliver practice training/assessment sessions. The scenarios should cover the different training/assessment, using a range of different training/assessment methods, while practice sessions should be structured around technical and non-technical markers with detailed feedback provided. Train the trainer/assessor sessions can be used for initial and refresher training, with the scenarios used for initial and ongoing assessment of competence.	

Table I.2: Example methods for training and assessing CRO trainers and assessors (continued)

Method	Description of train the trainer methods	Description of train the assessor methods
Delivery of training under supervision	Provide trainers/assessors with opportunities to deliver training/ assessments under supervision from a qualified trainer/assessor. Responsibility for training/assessment should increase, and requirement for supervision decrease, as the competence enhances. This transition should occur at an appropriate pace that is challenging, but does not overload or exceed the level of competence. Assessments of trainer/assessor competence, through observation, should be undertaken within this 'live' environment and can be used for initial and ongoing competence assessments.	
Ongoing mentoring and coaching	Provide new trainers/assessors with a mentor, to help them understand their role and provide target coaching to help support their ongoing development. Ongoing assessments of competence should be used to help structure this mentoring.	